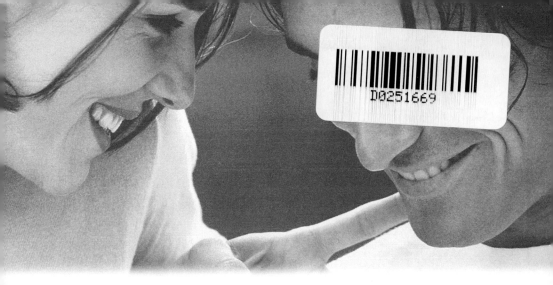

GENERAL EDITOR DENNIS RAINEY

preparing for marriage

BY DAVID BOEHI, BRENT NELSON
JEFF SCHULTE & LLOYD SHADRACH

BETHANYHOUSE
a division of Baker Publishing Group
Minneapolis, Minnesota

© 1998, 2010 by FamilyLife

Published by Bethany House Publishers
11400 Hampshire Avenue South
Bloomington, Minnesota 55438
www.bethanyhouse.com

Bethany House Publishers is a division of
Baker Publishing Group, Grand Rapids, Michigan

Bethany House edition published 2014
ISBN 978-0-7642-1550-6

Previously published by Regal Books

Printed in the United States of America

The Library of Congress has cataloged the original edition as follows:
    Preparing for marriage / David Boehi . . . [et al.] ; Dennis Rainey.
       p. cm.
    ISBN 978-0-8307-4640-8 (trade paper)
    1. Marriage—Religious aspects—Christianity. I. Boehi, David. II. Rainey, Dennis
  BV835.P73 2010
  248.4071—dc22   2010002991

18   19   20   21   22   23   11   10   9   8   7   6

Contents

preparing the
groundwork

Introduction
by Dennis Rainey

Not long after I graduated from the University of Arkansas, one of my good friends came to me for counsel. She was dating a young man who happened to be my best friend, and I knew what was happening in that relationship. She wanted to marry him, but he was hot and cold, uncertain of whether he was willing to commit himself to her.

For some reason, I had doubts about whether they should marry. So when she asked me for advice, I told her a parable I had recently heard:

> A little boy named Johnny was playing marbles in his front yard. His uncle drove up and decided to play with the boy for a few minutes. Then the uncle reached into his pocket and pulled out a dime and a dollar. "Johnny," he asked, "would you like a dime today or a dollar next week?"
>
> Johnny's boyish eyes bounced back and forth between the shiny dime and the crisp greenback. He thought, *I could buy a bag of potato chips today, or I could wait until next week and buy a rubber ball*. He felt some hunger pangs, so he grabbed the dime, bought some chips and wolfed them down. They were delicious.
>
> A week passed, and when Johnny went out to play one afternoon, he noticed that every other boy in his neighborhood had a rubber ball. He wanted one real bad, so he rode his bicycle over to his uncle's house. "Hey, Uncle, how about that dollar you promised me?" Johnny asked. But his uncle looked down and said, "Johnny, last week I promised you a dime today or a dollar next week, and you made your choice. You can't have the dollar now."

When I finished that story, I asked the young lady, "Do you believe that God is big enough to give you someone else later on that you could love more that this guy?" She thought for a moment and nodded her head yes.

"Perhaps," I said, "God in His sovereignty knows that this young man you are dating is a dime, and He has a dollar for you later on."

Well, perhaps you've guessed the end of my story. That young lady, Barbara Petersen, decided not to marry my best friend. In fact, just over a year later, she became my wife. To this day, people find it hard to believe that I really had no mixed motives when she and I talked that day!

Once in a while, Barbara and I pull out our old wedding pictures and gaze in wonder at those youthful faces. There we are, posing with our families. Reciting our vows. Cutting the cake.

I remember the sense of relief I felt. We did it! Finally it was over! Physically, mentally and emotionally, we felt like we had completed something, and we had—a six-week engagement filled with so much activity that we hardly had time to rest.

Did we truly realize what we had just done? Did we have any idea what type of commitment we had just made and what it would mean?

In reality, our wedding was not the completion of engagement but *the beginning of a new life*. Yet we scarcely knew what that life would involve. There's so much we didn't know about this thing called marriage.

We started our life together with the same youthful idealism and ignorance typical of so many other couples. I suppose we believed we really wouldn't face many problems. We learned the hard way that building a solid marriage requires commitment, sacrifice and *work*.

A Late-Night Discussion

During our first year of marriage, for example, we lived in Boulder, Colorado, where the winters are cold and electric blankets are standard equipment for survival. I can recall how both of us enjoyed sliding into those toasty-warm sheets after the electric blanket had done its duty. For some strange reason, however, neither of us could remember to turn out all the lights. We would snuggle in, and Barbara would say, "Sweetheart, did you remember to turn out all the lights?"

So I would hop out of our comfy bed and run barefoot through the 55-degree apartment, turning off light after light (that Barbara had turned on). It didn't happen that often, so I didn't mind—until one night when I dropped into bed totally exhausted. Just as I slipped into the third stage of anesthesia, Barbara gave me a little poke and said, "Sweetheart, aren't you going to turn out the lights?"

I groaned, "Honey, why don't you turn out the lights tonight?"

Barbara replied, "I thought you would, because my dad always turned out the lights."

Suddenly, I was wide awake. It dawned on me why I had been suffering occasional minor frostbite for the past few months. And I shot back, "But I'm not your dad!"

Well, we stayed up a long time that night discussing expectations—what Barbara expected me to do (because her father had always done it), and what I expected her to do (no matter who had always done it!).

That was a relatively simple conflict to resolve. But I remember a more serious problem that arose during that same year as the starry-eyed excitement of our honeymoon slowly wore off and we began to awaken to the reality of our lifetime commitment.

Barbara was not quiet when we spent time together; in fact, she talked more than I did. But when we went to any type of party or large group function, I was the "life of the party" while she followed me around the room and hardly said a thing.

I remember feeling trapped. She seemed like an appendage attached to my side. One of the reasons I was originally attracted to Barbara was because she seemed strong in areas where I was weak, and vice versa. We made a good team. But somehow those things that once attracted me didn't feel the same anymore. We were just so *different.*

Meanwhile, Barbara was feeling trapped as well. But we weren't single anymore. We both lived in the same home. At one point, Barbara went into the bathroom and locked herself in, thinking, *What in the world am I going to do? I can't get away from this.*

This was an important fork in the road for our marriage. Each of us had to decide before God if we would accept each other in spite of our differences and imperfections.

We had made that commitment standing before a pastor on September 2, 1972, but now the implications of that commitment were staring us in the face.

Fortunately, we made the right decision—to accept each other by faith, knowing that God had called us together. For though we were not well prepared for marriage, one all-important truth governed our relationship from the beginning: We were both committed to walking with God and knowing His will for our lives. And that has made all the difference for us.

Preparing for a Marriage, Not a Wedding

Now you are thinking of beginning that same journey. You are either engaged or seriously contemplating marriage, and you're excited about the possibility of spending the rest of your life with this special person. Yet, if you're honest with yourself, you probably feel a tinge of apprehension as well.

No other human relationship can approach the potential for intimacy and oneness than that which can be found within the context of the marriage commitment. And no other relationship can bring with it as many adjustments, difficulties and even hurts.

There's no way you can avoid these difficulties; each couple's journey is unique. But there is much you can do to *prepare* for that journey.

In simple terms, the goal of *Preparing for Marriage* is to help you make the most thorough, comprehensive and in-depth preparations possible. In fact, it includes the type of material that Barbara and I wish we had known before our wedding.

Like any journey with the potential for great reward, there are difficulties and obstacles to overcome along the way. This workbook is designed to guide you and prepare you to move through those challenges.

Here is what you can expect from going through this workbook:

- ♥ You will discover the joy of knowing your fiancé(e) and also being known by your fiancé(e) at levels you never imagined.
- ♥ You will talk about things you never dreamed you would but always knew you should.
- ♥ You will know, apply and experience God's Word as it relates to engagement and marriage.
- ♥ You will be confident, certain and secure in your decision to marry (or even not to marry).
- ♥ You will practice and apply foundational skills you will need to build your marriage.
- ♥ You will acquire essential communication skills.
- ♥ You will understand the critical nature of core roles in marriage.
- ♥ You will learn about God's design for true sexual intimacy and "total message" communication.
- ♥ You will, hopefully, connect with a mentor couple who can assist and counsel you as you prepare to begin your journey.

Because we are committed to your success, we have not chosen the easy road in developing this workbook. You will be asked some tough questions, and you'll be given some tough advice. Your preconceptions about engagement, marriage, God and His

Word will be tested. And in the process, you will be challenged to peel back the curtain and let who you really are shine through.

Completing this workbook requires commitment—a commitment to make it a priority and schedule the time required; to complete the work, with integrity and honesty. Most importantly, it will require a commitment to see the process through when difficulties challenge you to bail out.

If this is your intention, take a moment now and sign the "Our Commitment" box. It will serve as a tangible reminder to you and your fiancé(e) that you believe your future marriage is worth your very best effort in premarital counseling now.

Discovery, risk, challenge, intimacy, commitment, truth— all of these and more are what make marriage the most incredible journey you could ever imagine. Get ready to laugh. Get ready to cry. Get ready to learn. And get ready to experience the joy of a relationship like you've never experienced before.

Dennis Rainey
President, FamilyLife

OUR COMMITMENT

I commit to completing this premarriage workbook thoroughly and honestly. I will do my best to complete the assignments. I will make certain that this process remains at the top of my priority list and schedule. And when the process is difficult, I will press on.

I undertake this pledge as a reflection of my commitment to my fiancé(e) and to our future marriage.

_____ Date _____

_____ Date _____

How to Use This Workbook

Preparing for Marriage includes the following components:

1. Opening Worksheets
   The workbook begins with two worksheets designed to help you learn more about each other and about what you expect from marriage:

   - ♥ **"Great Expectations"** helps you understand the way you picture marriage and what you expect from your fiancé(e).

   - ♥ The **"Understanding Your Personal History"** worksheet (page 19) includes dozens of questions designed to help you understand your past and share it with your fiancé(e).

2. The Main Chapters
   The eight chapters in this workbook are divided into three sections:

   - ♥ **"Laying the Foundation"** provides an overview of God's purposes and plan for marriage.

   - ♥ **"Making the Decision"** guides you through a process of evaluating your relationship and then understanding how to make a biblical decision about marriage.

♥ **"Building Oneness"** covers some basic "how-to" information on four critical areas of marriage: communication, roles and responsibilities, finances and sexual intimacy.

Here's what you will find in each chapter:

 True North is a statement of the biblical truth related to the topic you are covering.

 Get the Picture introduces the topic, providing opportunities to answer questions and complete exercises that allow you to grasp the topic and understand why it is important for you.

 Get the Truth examines biblical truths on God's principles about different aspects of marriage.

 Navigating by True North: Truths to Chart Your Course is a list of summary statements of the key principles from each chapter.

 Couple's Project is the interaction portion of the chapter. Each project includes the following sections:

 Get Real: Questions to guide your discussion.

 Get to the Heart of Your Marriage: An opportunity to pray together and experience a spiritual discipline that will be one of the keys to your growing marriage in the years to come.

Get Deeper: Optional assignments for the highly motivated—those who want to go where no engaged couple has gone before!

 Special Questions for Those Who Were Previously Married: This additional material should help you discuss some important topics and, perhaps, uncover some issues to be resolved before your new marriage.

3. Bonus Projects

In the appendix you will find two optional questionnaires that will significantly enhance the value of this workbook:

♥ The **"Parental Wisdom Questionnaire"** is a valuable opportunity to receive encouragement and wisdom from your parents and in-laws.

♥ The **"Couple Interview"** helps you get some advice from a couple with a good track record in marriage.

Two other notes regarding format: First, in order to receive the most benefit from this notebook, we strongly recommend that each person obtain a workbook. Second, the word "fiancé(e)" has been chosen to represent both the man or woman, as in "meet with your fiancé(e) to discuss your answers." We realize this word may feel a bit strange, but we figure you'll be able to overlook that awkwardness as you work through this study.

The Value of a Mentor

Completing this workbook together as a premarried couple will be a rich experience. But there's an even better alternative: The value of this workbook will increase exponentially when it is completed under the guidance of a mentor. This could be a pastor, a counselor, a layperson or even a lay couple. In fact, we've written a separate Leader's Guide that gives them the instruction they need to guide you through your premarital counseling.

You may have already arranged to meet with a pastor, counselor or married couple who will serve as mentors for this course. By giving you access to their lives, allowing you to ask questions, they can provide a model for how a satisfying marriage relationship can work. This mentoring relationship may have a greater impact than anything else you learn in this course.

If you have been planning to complete this workbook on your own, we encourage you to think of a godly couple who you respect and who have been married at least five years. Take the initiative to ask them to mentor you through your premarital counseling. Give them a copy of the Leader's Guide and ask them to invest in your future marriage by sharing theirs with you and your fiancé(e).

Time Required

To receive the maximum benefit from the workbook, we strongly suggest the following:

- ♥ Plan on beginning the course so that the last chapter is completed a minimum of four weeks prior to the wedding date.

- ♥ Set aside two weeks to complete the two opening worksheets, and then two weeks for each chapter. This will give you time to complete your assignments, meet together to discuss the material and process what you are learning and discovering. It will also give you time to make needed decisions and resolve any significant issues between chapters.

We estimate that most chapters should take about two hours to complete: an hour for each of you to complete "Get the Picture" and "Get the Truth" and another hour to complete the Couple's Project. Some chapters may take a bit longer.

Set aside plenty of time to complete the Special Couple's Projects. These are a key part of the workbook and are worth the effort! They also will give you plenty of topics for discussion.

Charting a Course for True North

Did you know that when you hold up a compass and the arrow points north, it's not really pointing to the North Pole?

The North Pole is the geographic top of the earth. It's a fixed position that never changes. That's why it is called "true north." And it is from this fixed position that mapmakers draw their maps.

Your compass, on the other hand, does not point to True North. Rather, it points to a magnetic field that is roughly 1,300 miles away from the North Pole. This is called "Magnetic North."

Here is the point: Every pilot and every sea captain must make constant adjustments from what a *compass* says is north and what the *map* says is true north. Failing to make this adjustment of even a few degrees early in the journey could mean missing the destination by hundreds of miles.

For someone searching for truth in today's world, true north is the truth of God's Word. It is fixed, certain and absolute. It is to life and marriage what the geographic North Pole is to a map of the earth.

Magnetic north, on the other hand, can be deceiving. The arrow on the compass is pointing to what the compass says is north. It feels right. It looks right. Yet it will not direct you to your desired destination.

In the world you will find many ideas of how to build a strong marriage, but most of those ideas cannot be trusted. In creating this workbook, our desire is to provide you a glimpse of what God's Word says about building a strong marriage. By navigating according to True North, you can look at the map, consider your destination, talk about the alternatives and decide how you want to navigate your journey.

Understanding Your Personal History

One of the riskiest, but most rewarding benefits of a marriage relationship is the exhilarating experience of knowing and being known, of revealing and having another person reveal himself or herself to you. However, dating and even engagement can work against this process. On one hand, you want to know everything about this person. On the other hand, you think if this person knew everything about you, he or she might lose interest!

You may think you know your fiancé(e) better than anyone else on earth. But we want to help you deepen that knowledge, beginning with this worksheet that guides you through a discussion about your past and how it affects you today.

The past shapes all of us in ways we rarely understand. Your past influences your behavior, your personality, your emotions, your opinions and convictions. You and your fiancé(e) have probably not attempted to conceal your background from each other. But you may not have taken the time needed to adequately examine how your past influences your future.

For example, when most couples marry today, they assume that their marriage is between two people who want to become one. In reality, it is two people and *two families* that are coming together to form a new merger. Your family's impact on your new family must not be minimized, but rather, understood, and planned for.

We estimate this project will take at least two hours to complete, but you will find the effort well worth it. As you complete this project, you'll uncover some treasures along the way that will enrich your current relationship. You'll also locate a few old rusty nails that if not properly handled could create wounds that will infect your future marriage.

Take your time and answer each question as thoroughly as possible. You will give a copy of this project to your pastor, counselor or mentor couple.

NAME: _____ AGE: _____

FIANCÉ(E)'S NAME: _____ AGE: _____

Current Occupation: _____

Length of employment at my current job: _____
Highest level of education completed: _____
Hobbies and interests: _____
_____
_____
_____
_____

Previously married?　❒ No　❒ Yes　How many times? _____

❒ Divorced　❒ Widowed

How long have you been divorced or widowed? _____

Section One: Your Relationship History

Your Current Relationship

1. How we met

   _____

   _____

   _____

   _____

   _____

   _____

2. What attracted me to him/her

   _____

   _____

   _____

   _____

   _____

3. How long we have been dating

   _____

   _____

   _____

   _____

Your Friendships

4. Friendships for me have generally been (check one)

   ❑ Easy . . . like falling off a log
   ❑ So-so . . . I can take 'em or leave 'em
   ❑ A challenge . . . a lot of work but satisfying and
     rewarding
   ❑ Discouraging . . . more pain than I bargained for
   ❑ Absent . . . I've never really had a truly close friend

Explain why you checked the box you did:

_____
_____
_____
_____
_____
_____
_____
_____

5. Who are two of your closest friends, and what makes those relationships significant or special?

_____
_____
_____
_____

   How long have they been your friends?

_____
_____

6. What are three to five words these friends would use to describe you?

_____
_____

Past Dating Relationships

7. Describe a serious dating relationship from the past. Briefly state how it began, progressed and ended.

_____
_____
_____
_____
_____

8. Can you identify any patterns that seem to be present in your relationships with the opposite sex? (Examples: "My tendency is to 'fall in love' hard and fast, then get hurt" or "I am generally the more committed person in my relationships.")

For Previously Married Only

If you are divorced:

1. Why did you get a divorce? What were your reasons for divorcing?

---

2. Have you sought reconciliation with your former spouse? If so, how? If not, why not?

---

3. Have you discussed with your pastor or counselor whether you are free to remarry from a biblical standpoint? Write down your conclusion:

---

4. Give three reasons you may be confident you have gotten over your previous marriage and are ready to remarry:

_____

_____

_____

_____

_____

5. If you are unsure, explain why.

_____

_____

_____

_____

Section Two: Your Family

Home Environment

1. How would you describe your childhood?

_____

_____

_____

_____

What was best about your childhood?

_____

_____

_____

_____

What was most difficult?

_____

_____

_____

_____

2. What was your family's socio-economic background as you were growing up? What is it now?

_____

_____

_____

_____

_____

3. How would you describe the emotional environment of the home you grew up in?

_____

_____

_____

_____

_____

4. Did you experience any type of abuse (physical, emotional, sexual) as you grew up? Explain.

_____

_____

_____

_____

_____

5. What hardships (traumatic events, financial difficulties, and so on) has your family experienced?

_____

_____

_____

_____

_____

6. As you look back over your family history, do you see any legacies that have been passed from one generation to the next? (For example, one family might pass on a tradition of trusting God in tough circumstances, while another

family might pass on a tendency toward turning to alcohol to alleviate problems.)

_____

_____

_____

_____

Parents

7. What words would you use to describe your parents' marriage? Tell why you chose each word.

   _____

   _____

   _____

   _____

8. As parents, what did your dad and mom do well?

Dad	Mom

9. As parents, what do you wish they would have done differently?

Dad	Mom

10. Describe the most significant impact your parents have had on you (positive or negative).

Dad	Mom
_____	_____
_____	_____
_____	_____
_____	_____
_____	_____

11. What roles did your parents assume in the household?

_____

_____

_____

_____

_____

Who was the leader in the marriage?

_____

_____

_____

Who was the leader as a parent?

_____

_____

_____

How did they make decisions?

_____

_____

_____

12. Choose three or more words to describe your relationship with your father, and tell why you chose them.

    _____

    _____

    _____

    _____

13. Choose three or more words to describe your relationship with your mother, and tell why you chose them.

    _____

    _____

    _____

    _____

14. In what ways are you similar to each of your parents?

    _____

    _____

    _____

15. In what ways are you different?

    _____

    _____

    _____

16. Are there any unresolved issues between you and your parents? Articulate them here if you can.

    _____

    _____

    _____

    _____

17. What are your parents feeling about your choice of a spouse?

    _____

    _____

    _____

    _____

Siblings and Other Relatives

18. Rate your relationship with each of your siblings:

	Distant			Close	
Sibling: _____	1	2	3	4	5
Sibling: _____	1	2	3	4	5
Sibling: _____	1	2	3	4	5
Sibling: _____	1	2	3	4	5
Sibling: _____	1	2	3	4	5
Sibling: _____	1	2	3	4	5

19. Describe any special and unique relationships you have with other relatives (grandparents, aunts, uncles, cousins).

_____

_____

_____

_____

_____

_____

Section Three: Your Spiritual Journey

20. What kind of religious upbringing did you have?

_____

_____

_____

_____

21. What role does God play in your life today?

_____
_____
_____
_____

23. How certain are you that you are going to heaven when you die?

☐ Absolutely certain
☐ Sort of certain
☐ Not certain at all

Why?

_____
_____
_____
_____

24. Describe your spiritual life over the past 10 years. What were the high points?

_____
_____
_____
_____

What were the low points?

_____
_____
_____
_____

What caused growth or prevented growth?

_____
_____
_____
_____

25. Check the areas of your life in which you find it difficult to trust God and give Him complete control:

☐ Sex   ☐ Critical spirit   ☐ Relationships
☐ Thought life   ☐ Self-confidence   ☐ My future
☐ Worry   ☐ Finances   ☐ Anger
☐ Career   ☐ Decision making ☐ Relationship
                                                                  with parents

☐ Other_____

26. How has your involvement in a local church helped you grow in your relationship with Christ and in your outreach to others?

_____
_____
_____
_____

Section Four: Miscellaneous Topics

27. What has been your history in handling finances?

_____
_____
_____
_____

What are your strengths and weaknesses in handling money?

_____
_____
_____
_____

What type of debt do you currently have?

_____
_____
_____

28. What types of health (physical or mental) issues have you dealt with in the past?

_____

_____

_____

_____

What types of issues are you dealing with currently?

_____

_____

_____

_____

29. What have been your biggest successes at work?

_____

_____

_____

_____

30. What have been your biggest challenges at work?

_____

_____

_____

_____

31. What are the most courageous things you've ever done?

_____

_____

_____

_____

32. What have been your greatest triumphs in life?

_____

_____

_____

_____

33. What have been your greatest disappointments in life?

_____

_____

_____

_____

_____

Section Five: Your LifeMap

If you were to draw out your life from birth to this day, you would have before you a map of sorts. It would show where you started, the turns you've made along the way, the rivers you've crossed, the mountains you've climbed. You may even show where you drove off the road, suffered an accident or maybe had a flat tire along the way.

This project is designed to help you draw that map—for your benefit and your fiancé(e)'s. You'll both get a bird's-eye view of the major milestones that have shaped how you view yourselves and the world around you. The insights you gain into your own life and your fiancé(e)'s will deepen your understanding and appreciation of your unique relationship.

IMPORTANT NOTES:

1. This exercise is intended to give a summary view of your life. You will not be able to fit your whole "Life Story" into this project.

2. Complete your LifeMap privately. Do not interact with your fiancé(e) as you work on it.

3. You will not interact as a couple upon completing this LifeMap project. Keep your LifeMap confidential until chapter 4, when you will use it in a communication exercise.

Milestones

In this section you will answer questions to help you identify major milestones at different stages of your life. As you consider each period, consider things such as:

- ♥ Favorite teachers, coaches, Sunday School teachers, youth workers and others who shaped your view of yourself and the world
- ♥ Family events: vacations, traditions, tragedies, moves, secrets
- ♥ Hobbies and interests, sports, activities (Scouts, piano, tennis, and so on)
- ♥ Relationships: Close friends, sibling relationships, dating relationships
- ♥ Good and bad decisions you've made
- ♥ Spiritual highs and spiritual lows
- ♥ Goals accomplished and goals yet to be met
- ♥ Jobs you've had

Birth through elementary school

1. List at least three memories you can vividly recall about this period of your life.

_____

_____

_____

_____

Middle school through high school

2. List at least five events, circumstances or experiences that you think shaped your life during this period of your life.

_____

_____

_____

_____

_____

Post-high school to the present

3. List at least five significant events, circumstances or experiences from this period of your life.

_____

_____

_____

_____

_____

_____

Milestones to Mile Markers

Now you will turn these milestones in your life into mile markers on your own LifeMap. A mile marker tells you where you are, how far you've come and how far you have to go. Choose the milestones from the first section that you would like to plot on your LifeMap, and plot them at the appropriate spot.

Use the sample LifeMap below as a guide in developing your own. Here are the key things to remember:

- ♥ This is not meant to be an exhaustive life history. It should be a simple, clear overview of the major milestones in your life and how they affected you.

- ♥ The midline is emotional neutral. Anything above the midline indicates you found this to be a particularly enriching event/circumstance/experience. Anything below the midline indicates you found this to be particularly difficult or troubling.

- ♥ All of us have highs and lows in the normal ebb and flow of life. Points above and below the midline are not indicative of the value or quality of your life. They simply point out the major milestones of your life, how you view them and how they've influenced you.

(Try to plot at least 7, and no more than 12, mile markers.)

Sample LifeMap

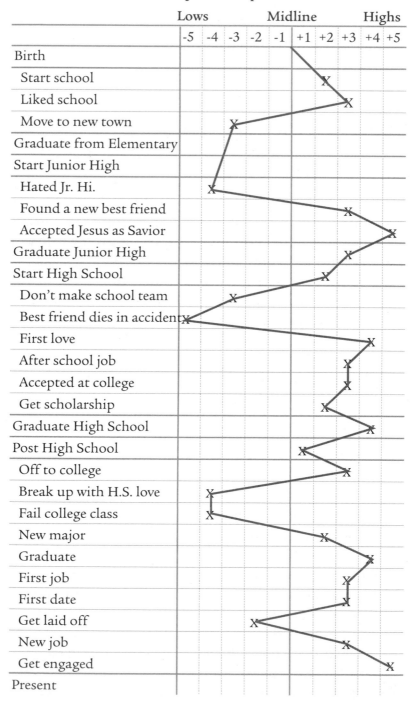

	Lows					Midline		Highs		
	-5	-4	-3	-2	-1	+1	+2	+3	+4	+5
Birth										
Start school										
Liked school										
Move to new town										
Graduate from Elementary										
Start Junior High										
Hated Jr. Hi.										
Found a new best friend										
Accepted Jesus as Savior										
Graduate Junior High										
Start High School										
Don't make school team										
Best friend dies in accident										
First love										
After school job										
Accepted at college										
Get scholarship										
Graduate High School										
Post High School										
Off to college										
Break up with H.S. love										
Fail college class										
New major										
Graduate										
First job										
First date										
Get laid off										
New job										
Get engaged										
Present										

Your LifeMap

	Lows					Midline			Highs	
	-5	-4	-3	-2	-1	+1	+2	+3	+4	+5
Birth										
Graduate from Elementary										
Start Junior High										
Graduate Junior High										
Start High School										
Graduate High School										
Post High School										
Present										

Great Expectations

Expectations are so basic that we often don't even recognize them, yet they influence our behavior every day—how we treat people, how we react to different situations.

Each of us brings a certain set of expectations in a marriage. We have a mental picture of how we will live and behave and interact. These expectations range from the routine to the profound—from dividing household responsibilities to determining who will take spiritual leadership in the home.

For example, H. Norman Wright notes in his book *Communication: Key to Your Marriage*:

> Too many couples enter marriage blinded by unrealistic expectations. They believe the relationship should be characterized by a high level of continuous romantic love. As one young adult said, "I wanted marriage to fulfill all my desires. I needed security, someone to take care of me, intellectual stimulation, economic security immediately—but it just wasn't like that!" People are looking for something "magical" to happen in marriage. But magic doesn't make a marriage work: hard work does.[1]

Buried expectations can poison a relationship. Unresolved expectations often lead to demands, and demands lead to manipulation. One person maneuvers the other to meet the expectation, while the other tries to avoid it. Inevitably, this leads to isolation in marriage, with two people playing absurd but dangerous games in an attempt to establish control.

While many of your own expectations about marriage will inevitably remain buried until after you are married, there is great value in discussing some of them now. In the process you should learn how to deal with differing expectations so they will not cause disappointment and disillusionment in your relationship.

Fantasy and Reality

1. What do you think of each of the following statements?

   a. "These feelings of love and passion will never fade after we are married."

   b. "Life will always be exciting after we are married."

   c. "If I get married, I will no longer be lonely."

   d. "My mate will meet all my needs."

   e. "If I get married, I will be able to help my mate become a better person."

   f. "My marriage will always be marvelous if I marry a Christian."

Each of these statements contains a large grain of truth, but these beliefs also could quickly lead to disappointment and disillusionment. Hard as it may be for you to believe, your feelings of love and passion *will* tone down a bit after marriage. Life will not always be exciting—remember that you're pledging to care for one another "for better or for worse" and "in sickness and in health."

Illusion and Reality
Some of our expectations are based on a fantasy of romance and marriage that our culture often promotes.

2. Do you think any of these statements about "fantasy marriage" ring true for your relationship? Explain.

_____

_____

_____

_____

A Guiding Principle

As you begin to identify and discuss your expectations, Philippians 2:3-4 provides a principle that should govern your attitudes:

> Do nothing from selfishness or empty conceit, but with humility of mind regard one another as more important than yourselves; do not merely look out for your own personal interests, but also for the interests of others.

3. Complete the following statement:

When one of my expectations is not met, I should . . .

_____

_____

_____

_____

The Christian life is ultimately "other" focused, not "me" focused. The aim of our lives is to meet the needs of others. This means that our expectations, many of which are legitimate, must often be put aside for the needs of others. That is what Christ called "dying to self."

Discussing Expectations
Complete your Great Expectations survey individually, and then meet with your fiancé(e) to discuss your answers. Here are a few suggestions for your discussion:

♥ *Identify* where the expectation came from: Is this a product of my background, education, culture or personality?

♥ *Discuss* why the expectation is important to you and how you can express it in a non-demanding way.

♥ *Resolve* together how this expectation can be:

- Accepted and met by your fiancé(e)
- Adjusted so that it is reasonable
- Abandoned as unrealistic

This project should help you identity both realistic and unrealistic expectations. This can be like mining for precious ore. You may have to move tons of earth to get ounces of gold, but those priceless nuggets are well worth the effort it takes to find them. In the same way, many of our expectations are buried beneath a lifetime of conditioning, and we must work to uncover them.

Great Expectations Survey

Write down specific expectations you have for your marriage in the following categories. Write down how *you feel* about the particular item, not what you think your fiancé(e) wants to hear. Answer all the questions. The more specific and honest you are, the more "gold" you'll discover.

Marriage Relationship

1. How will you make decisions once you are married, and what will you do when you find that you cannot agree?

_____

_____

_____

_____

_____

2. How often do you expect to spend time with your friends after you are married?

_____

_____

_____

_____

_____

3. How will you relate to opposite-sex friends after you are married?

_____

_____

_____

_____

_____

Finances

4. Who will be the primary financial provider in the family?

_____

_____

_____

_____

5. Do you anticipate both husband and wife pursuing careers? If yes, for how long?

_____

_____

_____

_____

6. How will you decide on major purchases?

_____

_____

_____

_____

7. Who will pay the bills, balance the checkbook and keep track of expenses?

_____

_____

_____

_____

8. What is your philosophy of giving (charitable donations to your church or to other organizations) and how will you make decisions about giving?

_____

_____

_____

_____

9. What is your conviction about debt and the use of credit cards?

_____

_____

_____

_____

Home

10. Where do you want to live?

_____

_____

_____

In what setting would you want to live (i.e., city, suburb, small town, rural, plains, mountains, desert, coastal)?

_____

_____

_____

11. Do you want to live in an apartment or house? Will you rent or buy?

_____
_____
_____
_____

12. What do you expect your standard of living to look like after five years of marriage?

_____
_____
_____
_____

13. How soon after you are married do you expect to have your home reasonably furnished?

_____
_____
_____
_____
_____

Social/Entertainment/Home Environment

14. How important are family meal times to you? How often will you eat out?

_____
_____
_____
_____

15. Do you want a pet in the home? If so, what type?

_____
_____
_____
_____

16. How often do you want to invite people to your home?

_____

_____

_____

_____

What kind of entertaining do you expect to do (i.e., formal or informal dinner, lavish or simple parties, and so on)?

_____

_____

_____

_____

_____

17. How often will you go out on dates?

_____

_____

_____

_____

18. What will be the role of television in your home, and what guidelines will you have about what you watch?

_____

_____

_____

_____

_____

How often do you expect to watch favorite programs or attend sporting events?

_____

_____

_____

_____

19. What will be your guidelines about movies?

_____

_____

_____

_____

_____

20. How do you think your friendships with other people will change after marriage?

_____

_____

_____

_____

_____

21. What hobbies or recreational pursuits will you pursue individually?

_____

_____

_____

_____

_____

Together?

_____

_____

_____

_____

_____

How often will you pursue them?

_____

_____

_____

_____

_____

22. How do you feel about drinking alcohol, or having alcoholic beverages in your home?

_____

_____

_____

Household Responsibilities

23. Who will prepare each meal, and what types of food will you eat?

_____

_____

_____

24. How clean do you want your home to be? What does "clean" look like to you?

_____

_____

_____

25. Who will do each of the following?

Laundry and ironing _____
Purchasing groceries _____
Automobile maintenance _____
Home repairs and yard work _____
General household cleaning _____
Cleaning bathrooms _____
Making the bed _____

Children and Parenting

26. What is your attitude toward children?

_____

_____

_____

27. When will you begin having children, and how many would you like to have?

28. What would you do if you cannot conceive biological children of your own?

29. What is your view on abortion?

30. What is your view on birth control?

31. Who will be the primary nurturer/caregiver of your children?

32. How will you discipline your children? How do you envision sharing that responsibility?

Spiritual

33. When and how often will you pray and study the Bible together?

_____
_____
_____
_____

34. Where will you attend church and what will your involvement be?

_____
_____
_____
_____

35. In what ways do you anticipate reaching out to others as a couple?

_____
_____
_____
_____

36. Who will take spiritual leadership in the home, and what do you think this means?

_____
_____
_____
_____

Holidays/Vacations/Special Occasions

37. Where will you spend Christmas, Thanksgiving and Easter?

_____
_____
_____

How will you decide?

_____
_____
_____

38. What expectations do you have for celebrating holidays?

_____
_____
_____

39. What will you do during your vacations?

_____
_____
_____

40. How will you celebrate birthdays and wedding anniversaries?

_____
_____
_____
_____

41. How much will you spend on gifts for family, friends and each other?

	Family	Your Children	Friends	Each Other
Birthdays?	_____	_____	_____	_____
Christmas?	_____	_____	_____	_____
Weddings?	_____	_____	_____	_____
Anniversaries?	_____	_____	_____	_____

42. What will you do on your weekends?

_____
_____
_____
_____

Parents and Other Relatives

43. How do you think your relationship with your parents will change after you are married?

_____

_____

_____

_____

44. How much time do you anticipate spending with your parents and your in-laws?

_____

_____

_____

_____

45. What type of relationship do you expect to have with your parents and your in-laws after marriage?

_____

_____

_____

_____

46. What other relatives (siblings, aunts, uncles, cousins) do you expect to be involved with in your marriage and family? In what ways would they be involved?

_____

_____

_____

_____

47. How involved do you want your parents and in-laws to be in your children's lives?

_____

_____

_____

_____

How will you accomplish this?

_____

_____

_____

_____

_____

Sex

48. What are your expectations about sex on your honeymoon?

_____

_____

_____

_____

_____

49. In your first year of marriage, how often do you expect to experience sexual intimacy?

_____

_____

_____

_____

50. What do you feel about your spouse sometimes saying "no" to having sex?

_____

_____

_____

_____

_____

51. What about sex during the wife's menstrual cycle?

_____

_____

_____

_____

Special Section for Those Who Have Been Previously Married

Marriage

1. Answer the following questions for each category below:

   ♥ Are you holding on to any unique expectations from your previous marriage?

   ♥ What do you expect to be different from your previous marriage?

   Marriage relationship:

   _____

   _____

   _____

   _____

   Finances:

   _____

   _____

   _____

   _____

   Home:

   _____

   _____

   _____

   _____

   Housekeeping:

   _____

   _____

   _____

   _____

Children and parenting:

_____
_____
_____
_____
_____

Social/entertainment:

_____
_____
_____
_____

Spiritual:

_____
_____
_____
_____

Holidays/vacations/special occasions:

_____
_____
_____
_____

In-laws/relatives:

_____
_____
_____
_____

Sex:

_____
_____
_____

2. If your fiancé(e) needs to contact his or her former spouse (due to finances, business, in-laws, children, and the like), how do you want that to be handled?

_____

_____

_____

_____

Children (If Applicable)

3. What kind of relationship do you expect to have with your spouse's children?

_____

_____

_____

_____

4. What kind of relationship do you expect your new spouse to have with your children?

_____

_____

_____

_____

5. How will you handle the children's need to see your former in-laws (their grandparents) and other relatives?

_____

_____

_____

_____

6. What guidelines need to be developed in disciplining the children?

_____

_____

_____

_____

7. How will you handle disagreements with former spouses about how to raise the children?

_____

_____

_____

_____

_____

If you both have children, what kind of relationship do you expect them to have with each other?

_____

_____

_____

_____

_____

8. What are the financial burdens involved in raising the children? How will these be handled?

_____

_____

_____

_____

9. Will you have additional children? When? How many?

_____

_____

_____

_____

_____

Note
1. H. Norman Wright, *Communication: Key to Your Marriage* (Ventura, CA: Regal Books, 1974), from the introduction.

part two

laying the
foundation

The men that women marry, and why they marry them,
will always be a marvel and a mystery to the world.

HENRY WADSWORTH LONGFELLOW

Chapter 1

Why Marriage?

TRUE NORTH
Marriage is God's idea.

Why Are You Considering Marriage?

That may sound like a simple question, yet how you answer it may give you a strong indication of how much you know about this commitment you are considering.

Seneca, a Roman philosopher, once wrote, "You must know for which harbor you are headed if you are to catch the right wind to get you there." One problem in our culture today is that, when it comes to marriage, many couples choose to set sail for the wrong harbors.

They may set their sights on the *harbor of personal fulfillment*, for example. "If I get married, I'll feel joy and happiness until the end of my days." But what happens when those emotions are not as intense as they expected—or when they don't feel joy and happiness?

How about the *harbor of companionship*? "I can't stand the thought of living alone for the rest of my life." This is a common reason for getting married. But what happens if you get tired of your spouse's companionship?

Then there's the *harbor of sexual fulfillment*. "Marriage means that I can enjoy sex anytime I want and never feel guilty or fearful." What happens if you meet someone else a few years later who seems sexier and more exciting?

Some people get married because they land in the *harbor of social acceptance*: "My family and friends won't quit asking me, 'Is there someone special in your life?'" Their friends are getting married, the years are passing and they don't want to be left behind. And what happens a few years later when they look at the person they chose and think, *If I had waited, I could have found someone better.*

Many of your human needs are met through marriage, and you do find happiness, companionship and sexual fulfillment. But marriage is about much more than meeting your own needs.

You may not know that marriage was not designed by humans, but by God, at the inception of the human race. And His design is much more magnificent than anything we could have imagined.

In this chapter and the next, you will discover that the only safe, secure and sensible harbor is the one found in the Person and Word of God.

 # GET THE PICTURE

Read this case study, and then answer the questions that follow.

Case Study: the Story of Eric and Amanda

Act One: The Magical Meeting

Who would have ever thought that Eric, an athlete and outdoorsman, and Amanda, a refined Southern lady, would wind up falling in love? They met while skiing with groups of friends deep in the heart of the Rocky Mountains in Colorado. The moment Eric saw Amanda, he approached her and asked her out. Amanda was intrigued that someone would be so bold, and she agreed.

For the rest of the week they found themselves en-
thralled with each other's company. They skied together, dined together, sipped hot chocolate together
and talked about anything they could think of. It all
felt so natural, so easy, like they almost fit together.

Both Eric and Amanda had dated many others in
the past, and Eric had even been engaged. But somehow they knew this relationship was different. After
the conference, they returned to their homes, which
were 300 miles apart; Eric co-owned a landscaping
company, while Amanda sold pharmaceuticals. Over
the next few months they talked nightly on the phone,
often for hours. They wrote and text-messaged each
other regularly, and often sent creative gifts. They also
spent as many weekends together as they could.

ACT TWO: Getting Serious

It was natural for Eric and Amanda to think about
marriage. He was 28 and she was 26, and they had always felt this would be the time to settle down.

Eric believed that the most important thing to
know before he got married was that his future bride
would be compatible with him. He wanted to find
someone who was attractive and fun to be with. He
also desired a wife who enjoyed fishing, was willing to
give him the freedom to be with his buddies and could
cook and keep the house clean.

Amanda also had expectations about marriage
and her future spouse. She dreamed of marriage as a
wonderful, romantic adventure with the man she
loved. He would be sensitive, attractive and well organ-
ized, and would share the home responsibilities. He
would express his feelings, be a good listener and provide security. He would enjoy children as much as she
did and would make a loving, caring father.

Because they had strong feelings for each other, Eric and Amanda were more than willing during the dating relationship to please each other. Eric often would be very vulnerable when he talked with Amanda, telling her about his struggles and doubts as well as his victories. He was the supreme gentleman, he was very creative with his romantic gestures and he really cared about listening to what Amanda had to say. He even took her to the theater, which she loved. Amanda thought, *This is the man of my dreams. We're perfect for each other. We hardly even argue.*

Amanda had never gone fishing as a child, but now she found herself spending weekends at a lake, casting for bass with Eric. She would attend his softball games and even cheered for Eric's favorite basketball team on television. Everything seemed fun when they spent time together. And Eric could not believe his taste buds when he ate Amanda's cooking. He thought, *This woman is like me in so many ways, and she likes to do things for me.*

A Few Differences

Of course, no two people are alike, and that was the case with Eric and Amanda. Their families were quite different—Eric's dad was an auto mechanic, and his mother a waitress. Amanda's parents were divorced, but her father, a wealthy attorney, provided well for all of them. This wide gap in socio-economic background was most apparent in the uneasiness they felt when they visited their prospective in-laws.

Eric was a boisterous, outgoing man who loved to be around lots of people. Amanda was much more reserved; she enjoyed spending time with a few close friends but felt uncomfortable at a large party. She loved reading, while he watched television to relax.

Amanda was bothered a bit about the difference in their religious convictions. She attended her church regularly; her belief in God was important to her. Eric said he had never enjoyed church and didn't attend on his own. But he did seem to enjoy going with her when he visited on weekends. That gave Amanda hope that he would eventually change. Considering everything together, they seemed perfect for each other, she thought.

They were tired of being single, and they couldn't stand to be apart. They couldn't imagine spending life without each other. And so, while Amanda was enjoying a traditional Fourth of July weekend with her family at a lake resort, she looked out one evening and saw, to her surprise, that Eric was standing by the lake. She ran out to greet him, and he dropped to his knees, held up a diamond ring and asked, "Will you marry me?"

They were engaged four months—just enough time to arrange the wedding. The final weeks were hectic: Amanda moved to Eric's city and started a new job while also setting up the wedding in her hometown . . . they met with Amanda's pastor and received some advice about marriage . . . they found a home and began moving in . . . and finally the big day arrived. The ceremony went by in a blur, and suddenly they found themselves reciting their vows: "With this ring I thee wed . . . in sickness and in health, in poverty or in wealth, 'til death do us part."

They headed off on their honeymoon certain they would live happily ever after.

1. What do you think about Eric and Amanda's decision to get married? Was it wise, or not?

_____

_____

_____

_____

2. If they had approached you and asked, "Do you think we are ready to get married?" how would you have answered?

_____

_____

_____

_____

_____

3. What were their reasons for getting married?

_____

_____

_____

_____

_____

 # GET THE TRUTH

In many ways, Eric and Amanda may be a superb match. Yet there was much they did not know about each other, and most of the time before they married was spent hundreds of miles apart. They were so caught up in a whirlwind of emotions that they failed to work out some crucial issues before they committed their lives to each other.

For one thing, there was much they still did not know about each other. Their family backgrounds were quite different, and the fact that Amanda's parents were divorced means that she grew up without a good model of how to build a successful marriage. They also had not really discussed philosophical or religious viewpoints to assess their compatibility on some of the deeper issues of life.

Their expectations about marriage were different; in fact, they seemed to have different goals in mind as they approached marriage.

In a sense, they were beginning marriage in the dark. And that's common of many couples today. They don't really know what marriage is about, and they know little about how to keep a marriage together.

Marriage is much more than a convenient pairing of man and woman. If we are to discover the answer to the question "Why marriage?" then we must go back to its origins and discover what was in the mind of its Creator. And to do that we must go back to the book of beginnings, the book of Genesis. It is here that we will discover God's purpose and plan for marriage.

Purpose Number One: Mutually Complete One Another

In the second chapter of Genesis we pick up the creation story after God has created man: "Then the LORD God said, 'It is not good for the man to be alone; I shall make him a helper suitable for him'" (Gen. 2:18).

Up to this point, God said everything He created was good. Yet here, by God's own declaration, we see that something is "not good."

1. Why do you think it wasn't good for Adam to be alone?

   _____

   _____

   _____

   _____

In the garden, Adam walked and talked with God. Yet that was not enough. God chose to create a unique need of *aloneness* in Adam that was not filled by His personal presence. Adam experienced God in the midst of perfection, yet Adam was *alone*.

2. Continue reading in Genesis to see what God did to solve Adam's problem:

   And out of the ground the LORD God formed every beast of the field and every bird of the sky, and brought them to the man to see what he would call them; and whatever the man called a living creature, that was its name. The man gave names to all the cattle, and to the birds of the sky, and to every beast of the field, but for Adam there was not found a helper suitable for him. So the LORD God caused a deep sleep to fall upon the man, and he slept; then He took one of his ribs, and closed up the flesh at that place. The LORD God fashioned into a woman the rib which He had taken from the man, and brought her to the man (Gen. 2:19-22).

a. Why do you think Adam could not find a "suitable" helper?

☐ None of the animals understood football.
☐ Adam snorted like a buffalo but he couldn't keep up with the herd.
☐ Adam was interested in the gorilla, but her breath could peel a banana.
☐ Like many men, Adam was keeping his options open.
☐ God was showing Adam his need for a mate.
☐ Other: _____

b. What did God do to address Adam's need for companionship?

_____
_____
_____
_____

Notice that God did much more than give Adam someone so that he wouldn't be lonely. God's solution for Adam's need was to "make him a helper suitable for him." It's important here to note that "helper" does not mean "inferior person." On the contrary, in the day when Moses penned these words, to identify a woman as a "helper" ran countercultural to the common low view of women. Moses actually elevated the sense of a woman's worth and role by calling her by the same name used in other places in the Old Testament to describe God Himself (see Pss. 30:10 and 54:4). To be called a "helper" here speaks more to the simple fact that God had plans for Adam that he could not fulfill without a mate—he was incomplete. Adam needed Eve.

Also notice that this passage does not imply that every un-married person is incomplete without a spouse. All of us are created in the image of God (see Gen. 1:26-27) and bring glory to God when we yield ourselves to His purpose and plan for our lives. (Jesus, after all, was single.) However, in God's tim-ing, He does sovereignly choose to bring a husband and wife together for them to accomplish together what they couldn't have accomplished apart.

When God calls you to marry, *He gives you a spouse who, by divine design, will complete you.* Together you will be stronger and more effective than when you were apart.

3. Think of some married couples you know well. In what ways do their differences complete each other?

_____

_____

_____

_____

_____

_____

Most happily married couples could point to specific exam-ples of how God has "fit" them together:

♥ The husband may be people-oriented, and his wife is task-oriented (or vice versa). He helps her relate so-cially to others; she keeps him focused on tasks they need to complete.

♥ He may run through life at a fast pace, while her inner clock impels her to move much slower. He helps her make it on time to meetings, while she helps him stop and smell the roses.

In His wisdom, God brings two people together to balance each other, to fill each other's gaps. They are stronger as a team than they were as individuals. They are two independent people who choose to become *interdependent*.

4. As you look at your relationship, in what ways are you different and alike?

Alike	Different
_____	_____
_____	_____
_____	_____
_____	_____
_____	_____
_____	

5. Describe some ways that your differences and weaknesses make you stronger as an interdependent team.

_____

_____

_____

_____

6. If a couple does not see their differences as part of God's design and purpose for their marriage, how will those differences challenge their relationship over time?

_____

_____

_____

_____

_____

It is your commitment to God—to know Him, to grow in your relationship with Him, to obey Him and follow His leading in your life—that will enable you to see your spouse as His perfect complement to your life.

Purpose Number Two: Multiply a Godly Legacy

As we continue looking at the book of Genesis, we find the second purpose of marriage:

> God blessed them; and God said to them, "Be fruitful and multiply, and fill the earth" (Gen. 1:28a).

7. This passage makes it clear that, according to God's design for marriage, having children is not an option, but a command. What do you think God had in mind when He made bearing children such a priority?

   _____

   _____

   _____

   _____

   _____

   _____

   _____

8. What do the following passages from Psalms tell us about God's opinion of children and why they are important to Him?

   > Behold, children are a gift of the Lord; the fruit of the womb is a reward. Like arrows in the hand of a warrior, so are the children of one's youth. How blessed is the man whose quiver is full of them; they shall not be ashamed when they speak with their enemies in the gate (Ps. 127:3-5).

For He established a testimony in Jacob and appointed
a law in Israel, which He commanded our fathers that
they should teach them to their children, that the generation to come might know, even the children yet to
be born, that they may arise and tell them to their children, that they should put their confidence in God and
not forget the works of God, but keep His commandments (Ps. 78:5-7).

_____
_____
_____
_____
_____
_____

Not only are children an incredible blessing (see Ps. 127), but
they also are a key part in God's plan. It is important to note that
these passages say nothing about how many children to have,
and we also realize that not every couple is able to have biological children of their own. But part of God's intent is for every
married couple to be ministering down into the next generation—passing on their faith in God so the next generation can
in turn pass it on to the next. Psalm 78 makes it clear that the
family is one of the best environments in which this can happen.

9. God could use any method He wanted to tell people about
   Himself (consider the shouting stones in Luke 19:40). So
   why do you think He places such great emphasis on fathers and mothers passing on truth to their children?

_____
_____
_____
_____
_____
_____

God's original plan called for the home to be a sort of greenhouse—a nurturing center where children grow up to learn character, values and integrity. In no other setting does a child learn more about how to live and relate to his God.

Purpose Number Three: Mirror God's Image

" 'Let Us make man in Our image, according to Our likeness; and let them rule over the fish of the sea and over the birds of the sky and over the cattle and over all the earth, and over every creeping thing that creeps on the earth.' God created man in His own image, in the image of God He created him; male and female He created them" (Gen. 1:26-27).

This third purpose for marriage—that God created it to mirror His image—is a critical foundation for understanding God's design. It means that God chose to reveal to us a part of His character and being through our relationships. For example, God is love; therefore, we can love. When we forgive each other, we reflect Him who forgave us in Christ (see Eph. 4:32).

Why is this important? Because God created us to know Him and to live within the context of His plan for our lives. When a man and woman come together in a marriage, with God at the center of their relationship, they will reflect His image. The world will see in that relationship a representation of who God is and how He loves.

Mysteriously, God chose to use a husband and wife to represent, or mirror, Him to humankind. It is through this marriage relationship that a couple *can* demonstrate a portion of God's love, His forgiveness and His longsuffering commitment to people.

10. List some ways that your marriage can mirror God's image. Review the sample answer to spark your thinking, and then write your own.

We mirror God's...	To each other	To others
Perfect love	when we believe the best about each other.	when we accept people as they are in spite of their weaknesses and faults.
Commitment		
Forgiveness		
Unity (Father, Son, Holy Spirit)		

Summary

Marriage is far more than a cultural institution or an arrangement for a man and woman to meet their needs for companionship. As we consider the purposes of marriage, we find the answers in the authoritative bestseller of all time, the Bible. All three of these purposes for marriage point us back to God, the spiritual originator of marriage. As Psalm 127:1 tells us, "Unless the LORD builds the house, they labor in vain who build it."

That means marriage is far more important than you may have thought. There is more at stake in your marriage than just two people enjoying each other's companionship and partnership. God's reputation—His image—is at stake in your marriage. To build a marriage according to God's design, you cannot ignore its spiritual foundation. And in the next chapter, we'll learn more about that foundation.

Why marriage? If you cannot answer this question, you will find yourself easily sidetracked and quite possibly permanently lost. But if you can answer it biblically, you will find the course to what we call a "oneness marriage," a remarkable and wondrous journey.

NAVIGATING BY
TRUE NORTH
Truths to Chart Your Course

♥ It's important to know why you are getting married.

♥ God created marriage so that two people would become one to accomplish three things:

1. Mirror His image
2. Mutually complete one another
3. Multiply a godly heritage

♥ You complete each other through your unique differences and weaknesses.

♥ The family is a greenhouse for spiritual growth and a relay center for passing on spiritual truths to the next generation.

♥ In marriage the world sees a picture of what God is like.

Couple's Project

 GET REAL

Interact as a couple on the following activities:

1. Spend a few minutes discussing the "Get the Picture" and "Get the Truth" sections, sharing your answers to the questions with each other.

2. Try this object lesson with your fiancé(e):

   a. Place your hand against that of your fiancé(e)'s opposite hand, keeping your fingers together. You will have come together to make "praying hands." This is a picture of the bond that your similarities create. How easy is it to break this bond? It's effortless; just pull your hands away.

   b. Now place your hands together again, this time with your fingers spread out. Let your fingers fill the gaps in your spouse's fingers and clasp down. This is a picture of what differences and weaknesses do in your relationship. They complement each other. They fill each other's gaps. Now, keeping your fingers wrapped, try to separate your hand from your fiancé(e)'s. It's difficult because in completing one another, you strengthen your bond.

3. In light of Scripture, has your view of having and raising children changed? If so, how?

_____

_____

_____

_____

_____

If you have not fully discussed your thoughts about raising a family, this would be a good time.

When do you want to begin having children?

_____

_____

_____

_____

How many do you think you would like to have?

_____

_____

_____

_____

Do you feel ready to have children soon? Why or why not?

_____

_____

_____

_____

4. Is the idea that your marriage would be a "mirror of God's image" a new one to you? In what way?

_____

_____

_____

_____

5. Have you seen your relationship reflect God's glory to other people? If so, how?

_____

_____

_____

_____

GET DEEPER

Here are two special optional assignments for those who want to go deeper.

1. Read chapter 11 in *Staying Close*, by Dennis and Barbara Rainey. (This resource is available through FamilyLife at 1-800-FL-TODAY.)

2. Complete the "Parental Wisdom Questionnaire" found on page 234.

SPECIAL QUESTIONS
for Those Who Were Previously Married

1. Refer to your Understanding Your Personal History worksheet (see page 19) and discuss your answers to questions for the previously married in the section on Your Relationship History.

2. Answer the following questions individually (if applicable), then share your answers with your fiancé(e).

In what ways did your previous marriage fail to fulfill God's purposes for marriage?

_____

_____

_____

_____

Mutually completing one another:

_____

_____

_____

_____

Multiplying a godly legacy:

_____

_____

_____

_____

Mirroring God's image:

_____

_____

_____

_____

3. If you were divorced: As you look back now, what mistakes did you make that led to the split? In other words, what was your responsibility?

_____

_____

_____

_____

4. If either of you have children, rate their emotional receptivity to the idea of your re-marrying: (think through why each child feels the way he or she does)

	Negative			Positive	
	1	2	3	4	5

_____ (child's name)

Why?

_____

_____

| _____
 (child's name) | Negative
 1 2 3 | Positive
 4 5 |

Why?

_____

_____

| _____
 (child's name) | Negative
 1 2 3 | Positive
 4 5 |

Why?

_____

_____

| _____
 (child's name) | Negative
 1 2 3 | Positive
 4 5 |

Why?

_____

_____

4. What plans do you have for helping your children adjust to a potential new step-parent (and step-brothers and/or step-sisters)?

_____

_____

_____

_____

 A SPECIAL MESSAGE
for Those Who Were Previously Married

God's purposes for marriage point to the fact that God intends marriage to be a lifelong commitment between one man and one woman.

- ♥ Mutually completing one another involves becoming one flesh and experiencing "oneness" that is never to be divided. (You'll learn more about this in the next chapter.)

- ♥ Multiplying a godly legacy (having and raising children) is meant to be done in the context of a family with both parents present and involved.

- ♥ Mirroring God's image means mirroring the unity displayed in the Trinity: Father, Son and Holy Spirit never sever their relationship with one another.

If you are divorced, you need to make every effort over a period of time to restore your relationship with your spouse. We recognize there are extenuating circumstances in certain cases that make this improbable and, possibly, unwise. You must seek godly counsel to help you sort through your unique issues.

As you consider another marriage, we assume that you have clear biblical grounds for your divorce. This means that you have studied the biblical passages pertaining to divorce and have sought and accepted godly counsel. God *allows* divorce between a husband and wife, but He never prescribes it. You need to have a clear conscience that you are living under His allowance and have the freedom, biblically, to remarry.

There is no more lovely, friendly, and charming relationship,
communion, or company than a good marriage.

MARTIN LUTHER

Chapter 2

God's Equation for Marriage:

When One Plus One Equals One

 TRUE NORTH

God's plan for marriage involves four commitments
that are lived out over a lifetime in the power of the
Holy Spirit: receiving, leaving, cleaving and
becoming one flesh.

For thousands of years, rulers and wealthy landowners built large castles for protection from enemies. Over the years, however, those enemies devised many ingenious methods of piercing a castle's defenses. They built catapults to hurl missiles against the walls or over them. They used battering rams to break through a wall. They constructed towers on wheels and then moved the towers up to the castle wall to allow men to breach the walls.

And if none of those strategies worked, they turned to the siege; they surrounded the castle and prevented food, water and any other supplies from entering. After weeks and sometimes months, the castle's inhabitants were forced to surrender.

By the thirteenth century in England, castle designers had learned from the mistakes of previous generations. They included many ingenious defenses in their blueprints:

- The outer walls angled sharply outward at the bottom. This provided additional stability and also provided a defensive strategy: huge boulders dropped by castle defenders would bounce off the sloped bottom and hit the enemy.

- Arrow slits were installed in the walls and designed so that archers could aim their bows.

- Slots were left at the top of the outer walls so they could create "hoardings"—wooden structures that hung out beyond the walls that allowed defenders to aim straight down at the enemy.

- Huge storage areas were created to accumulate food that could sustain inhabitants of the fortress for months at a time.

- A well was dug within the inner ring of walls so that castle defenders would have an independent water supply.

As you seriously consider marriage, you should realize that you will be constructing a home that needs to withstand the catapults and battering rams of our twenty-first century culture. No doubt you've thought of this yourself as you look out and wonder how you can make your marriage work in a world where so many are ending in divorce. One reason many people are fearful of committing to marriage is they don't want to end up like their friends or parents.

God has a plan for marriage, however, and He offers proven blueprints for building a successful relationship that will last for a lifetime. To build a strong marriage and family, you and your fiancé(e) need to work from the same set of biblical blueprints.

 # GET THE PICTURE

Read the following case study, and then answer the questions that follow.

Case Study: The Continuing Saga of Eric and Amanda

The morning after they arrived at their honeymoon location, Amanda awoke with a stomach flu. She spent two full days in bed, while Eric found himself walking alone along a warm, romantic beach, wondering why he was even there, and whether this was some sort of omen of trouble to come.

Fortunately, Amanda recovered fully, and they were able to enjoy at least a few days of romance and intimacy. Within a few weeks of returning home and settling into their new lives, however, they began experiencing some tension.

Amanda was unhappy with her new job in a new city. A successful pharmaceuticals salesperson back home, now she found herself starting from scratch again, building up a customer base. She would arrive home exhausted and irritable. On top of that, Eric had expected her to earn more money—something closer to her salary before they were married. Now their finances were tighter than he wished.

Eric had always worked long hours, often not returning home until late in the evening. With Amanda living in another town during their engagement, this never mattered. Now, Amanda felt lonely in a new home. "I hardly know anybody here," she complained. Eric, meanwhile, felt Amanda didn't understand his need to work long hours in order to keep up with their seasonal workload at the landscaping company. "It won't be as bad during the winter," he explained.

What bothered Eric and Amanda most, however, were the changes they saw in each other after their marriage. During their courtship and engagement, for example, they hardly argued, but now they clashed with each other on a number of fronts—how they divided housework, the way they kept track of their finances, how they treated their in-laws.

Amanda found herself resenting the amount of work she was expected to do to keep up the house, even though they both worked. About all Eric did was take out the trash and handle any home repairs requiring a tool. He rarely helped cook or clean or wash clothes or anything, it seemed. "I feel like I do everything around here," Amanda said. "You never do your fair share."

They also discovered that their interests were more divergent than they had realized. One week, Eric asked if Amanda wanted to go fishing on the weekend and was stunned when she replied, "I really don't like fishing. Can't we do something else instead?"

"But I thought you loved fishing!" Eric said.

"I got tired of it. Isn't there anything else we can do?"

The following week, Amanda was just as surprised when she told Eric about a theatrical play she wanted to see, and he replied that he would rather just stay home and watch a movie.

It felt as if they got lazy after reaching their goal of finding a spouse. They didn't talk like they once did. The spark was gone.

Amanda was disappointed that Eric didn't meet up to the type of man she thought he would be. She was surprised at how selfish he was at times. He didn't seem to care about her the way he once did. Eric was disturbed by Amanda's growing independence and antagonism; in fact, as he learned more about her divorced parents, he realized she treated him in much the same way her mother treated her father. He was puzzled that she had become so self-centered since their wedding day.

Perhaps, they thought, they just weren't compatible. Perhaps it was just a big mistake.

1. Why do you think Eric and Amanda became disillusioned so quickly after marriage?

   _____

   _____

   _____

   _____

2. What could they have done before they were married to make the transition easier?

   _____

   _____

   _____

   _____

 # GET THE TRUTH

If you were to describe the world's blueprints for marriage, it probably would be titled, "The 50/50 Relationship." This is how most people think of marriage, and on the surface it sounds reasonable: "If I do my part, and he does his, we'll meet each other halfway."

This plan is destined for failure, however, because:

♥ It does not take unrealistic expectations into account.
♥ It fails to anticipate the natural selfishness you both bring into a relationship.

When you consider these factors, you realize it is impossible to know if your spouse ever meets you halfway!

Fortunately, the Bible offers a better plan. Let's revisit the book of Genesis, where we will examine four commitments essential to building a marriage according to God's blueprints. Although the biblical principles for marriage are thousands of years old, we will discover that they are timeless, time-tested and relevant for our marriages today.

Commitment Number One: Receive Your Spouse

In Genesis 2:21-22, we read:

> So the LORD God caused a deep sleep to fall upon the man, and he slept; then He took one of his ribs and closed up the flesh at that place. The LORD God fashioned into a woman the rib which He had taken from the man, and brought her to the man.

Once God had made Adam "a helper suitable for him" (Gen. 2:18), one question remained: What would be Adam's response? Remember, he had been busy naming the animals when God used some celestial Sominex to put him under for rib surgery. No doubt, he had been dreaming of lions, tigers and bears, yet now before him was God's custom-made helper.

1. Put a checkmark by everything Adam knew about Eve when he first laid eyes on her:

   ❑ She could cook like his mom.
   ❑ One day she would inherit five million shares of Apple.
   ❑ Her voice reminded him of some feathery thing he named "bird."
   ❑ She really knew how to kiss.
   ❑ She liked to watch new movies (no black-and-white oldies).
   ❑ Other: _____

No, Adam didn't know anything about Eve—except that she had come from God.

2. So how did he respond?

> This is now bone of my bones and flesh of my flesh; she shall be called Woman, for she was taken out of man (Gen. 2:23).

The *Living Bible* paraphrase comes closest to capturing the real spirit of Adams's response: "This is it!" Another way to interpret the Hebrew here is, "Wow! Where have you been all my life?" In other words, Adam was excited—he was beside himself. (Pardon the pun!)

3. Why do you think Adam was so enthusiastic about a woman he didn't know?

   _____

   _____

   _____

   _____

This passage illustrates a cornerstone principle of marriage: Just like Adam, you must individually receive your spouse as God's provision for your need for companionship. You must accept His gift. Receiving your spouse demonstrates your faith in God's integrity.

Adam's focus was on God's flawless character, not on Eve's performance. He knew God, and he knew that God could be trusted. Adam enthusiastically received Eve because he knew she was from God. Adam's faith in God enabled him to *receive* Eve as God's perfect provision for him.

4. Complete the following sentence: If my fiancé(e) is God's provision for me, then receiving him or her as God's gift means that I should . . .

   _____

   _____

   _____

   _____

In marriage, you must receive your spouse in the same way Adam received Eve. If you decide your fiancé(e) is, indeed, God's provision, you need to accept your fiancé(e)'s strengths and weaknesses. Will you unconditionally accept good habits (that are known) and bad habits (that you haven't learned yet)? Will you look beyond physical attractiveness to the God who is the provider, who knows what He is doing?

In addition, receiving your spouse is not just a decision you make when reciting your wedding vows. It requires an attitude of *continual acceptance* throughout your marriage.

In the months and years after the wedding, each of you will become more and more aware of your respective weaknesses and faults. The more you remember your responsibility to receive each other as God's provision, the stronger your marriage will become. If the person who knows you best also loves you the most, your marriage will be truly special.

5. Consider the results of not continually receiving your spouse. Describe what would happen to such a marriage in 5 or 10 years.

_____

_____

_____

_____

Commitment Number Two: Leave Your Parents

Let's read on in the Genesis account to uncover more of God's blueprints for marriage:

> Therefore shall a man leave his father and his mother, and shall cleave unto his wife: and they shall be one flesh (Gen. 2:24, *ASV*).

As children, we are dependent upon our parents for the material and nonmaterial things in life. Our parents have the responsibility of providing food, shelter and clothing, as well as emotional stability, godly values and spiritual growth. But just as the doctor cuts the umbilical cord from the baby to the mother, so too you must cut the umbilical cord of *dependency* and *allegiance* from your parents. You should always honor your parents (see Exod. 20:12) but if you don't leave them in the spirit of Genesis 2:24, you will undermine the interdependence you are to build as husband and wife.

Leaving involves two kinds of surgery:

- ♥ Severing the cord of dependency. This means choosing not to rely on your parents for material or emotional support. You could say that the wedding day is to a man or woman what July 4 is to America—a declaration of independence.

- ♥ Severing the cord of allegiance. During the wedding ceremony, our priorities officially change. You should always honor your parents and remain committed to them. But your first and foremost loyalty is to your spouse.

6. In your own words, write a one-sentence definition of what the Bible means by "a man shall leave his father and mother."

_____

_____

_____

7. What are some common ways that individuals fail to cut the cord of dependence after they are married?

_____

_____

_____

8. What are some common ways individuals fail to cut the cord of allegiance?

_____

_____

_____

_____

9. In what ways do you think your parents, or your fiancé(e)'s parents, will find it difficult to let you "leave"?

_____

_____

_____

_____

Commitment Number Three: Cleave to Your Spouse

Genesis 2:24 tells us that after leaving his parents, a man shall "cleave to his wife." To "cleave" means to stick like glue. It is a permanent bond, not meant to be broken.

10. In a marriage relationship, the glue that keeps you to-gether is (pick one):

    ❐ Expectations of extended family to never get a di-vorce and mar the family name
    ❐ The IRS exemptions
    ❐ The need to keep a divorce from impeding my ca-reer track
    ❐ A vow/covenant—a commitment of my will to honor my word, my wife and my God
    ❐ Good communication and problem-solving skills

On your wedding day you will participate with your spouse in one of the most solemn pledges ever given to humankind—the vow of marriage. This vow, or covenant, is a lifelong commit-ment, a promise not just between two people but between a man and a woman and their God. It involves three promises:

    ♥ To stay married throughout your lives
    ♥ To love and care for each other
    ♥ To maintain sexual fidelity

One reason so many people divorce today is that they fail to enter into marriage with a firm commitment to not get a divorce. In the back of their minds, they figure they will find someone else if this relationship doesn't work out.

When you enter into marriage, you must do it with the understanding that you will keep your covenant. This sacred, unconditional commitment will create a secure marriage relationship. A partial commitment will only create fear and guarantee the failure of your marriage.

11. Read the following Scripture passages:

"Take heed then to your spirit, and let no one deal treacherously against the wife of your youth. For I hate divorce," says the LORD (Mal. 2:15-16).

Some Pharisees came to Jesus, testing Him and asking, "Is it lawful for a man to divorce his wife for any reason at all?" And He answered and said, "Have you not read that He who created them from the beginning made them male and female, and said, 'For this reason a man shall leave his father and mother, and be joined to his wife; and the two shall become one flesh'? So they are no longer two, but one flesh. What therefore God has joined together, let no man separate" (Matt. 19:3-6).

Why do you think God feels so strongly about divorce? (Think back on all you've learned so far about God's purposes and plans for marriage.)

_____

_____

_____

_____

Author Elisabeth Elliot has said, "Love is to will another person's good." It is not based on feelings or emotions. This idea is at the heart of commitment. Commitment is willing another person's good *through an unbreakable pledge of fidelity and devotion*. It is the unconditional, irrevocable promise to always be there. It is the resolute conviction of your will to stick to that person for life.

When you display that type of commitment in marriage, you truly fulfill God's purposes. And you become a witness to the world of God's character. Your unconditional commitment to each other mirrors God's unconditional commitment to you. Divorce not only causes terrible damage to you and to those you love, but it also brings shame upon the name of Christ.

Commitment Number Four: Become One Flesh

In the progression of Genesis 2:24, we see that a man shall leave his parents, cleave to his wife, and then become one flesh with his wife. Sexual intercourse consummates a marriage, binds a couple together and symbolizes the oneness they experience in their relationship. That is why we say that, in marriage, one plus one equals one!

Sexual intercourse is an integral part of becoming one flesh, but not the whole. Becoming one flesh involves *deep relational intimacy*. Here's what Christian psychologists Clifford and Joyce Penner write about the term "one flesh":

> [It] means far more than a mere physical meeting of bodies. The Scripture is talking about that mystical union between husband and wife that unites two people as total persons.
>
> Love-making cannot be just physical. . . . The total person—intellect, emotions, body, spirit, and will— becomes involved in the process of giving ourselves to each other.[1]

When you look at the place of "becoming one flesh" in God's plan for marriage, it is clear that it should *follow* commitment—

not precede it. It's receive, leave, cleave and *then* become one flesh. God's plan is for sexual relations to be enjoyed within the context of a committed marriage relationship (see Mark 7:21; Rom. 13:13; 1 Thess. 4:3).

In chapter 8 we will discuss the sexual union in more detail. But notice the progression (see Gen. 2:18-25) that God has established as His blueprint for building a relationship:

♥ Man is alone.
♥ He recognizes his need.
♥ God provides for this need.
♥ Man receives that provision.
♥ Both man and woman leave father and mother.
♥ They cleave to one another.
♥ They become one flesh.
♥ They experience intimacy and oneness.

As you and your spouse daily embrace God's purposes and plans for marriage, you will begin the process of becoming one. Something is born on every wedding day. Before the wedding ceremony, there is *he* and *she*. After the ceremony there is a new entity called "us." This is the one flesh God speaks of— a growing, thriving, living relationship. We call this "oneness."

When you and your fiancé(e) are both committed to receiving, leaving, cleaving and becoming one flesh—you are building from God's blueprint. Get ready for the divine mathematical mystery where one plus one equals one!

The Heart of a Oneness Marriage

When you build a marriage according to God's blueprint, you experience the benefits of living according to His plan. Ecclesiastes 4:9-10 tells us: "Two are better than one because they have a good return for their labor. For if either of them falls, the one will lift up his companion. But woe to the one who falls when there is not another to lift him up."

A "oneness marriage" is the opposite of the world's 50/50 plan. It is a 100/100 plan in which both husband and wife commit themselves totally to each other, set aside their own selfishness, and experience true intimacy. In the 100/100 plan, there is no talk about "meeting each other halfway." You are both willing to do anything it takes to make the marriage work.

In our discussion about God's purposes and plan for marriage, we've discussed some of the commitments you need to make to build a solid marriage. Everything we've learned points to one central fact: For your marriage to become what God intended it to be, you must make a commitment to put God at the center of your relationship. The heart of a oneness marriage is an intensely spiritual relationship between one man and one woman and their God. It demands a lifelong process of relying on God and forging an enduring relationship according to His design.

We'd like to challenge you with two questions that may be the most important you've ever considered:

Is Christ at the Center of Your Life?
To truly live according to God's purposes and plan for marriage, you need God's power. You need a relationship with Him.

Spiritually speaking, take a look in the mirror and analyze what you see:

- ♥ Have you ever received Christ as your Savior and Lord?

- ♥ Has God been at work in your life over the past couple of years?

- ♥ Are you growing in your relationship with Him?

If you have trouble answering any of these questions, we suggest reading "Our Problems, God's Answers" on page 245. You will learn more about how to experience a relationship with Christ.

Is God Calling You Together as Man and Wife?
This is the Million Dollar Question for any Christian couple
contemplating marriage. To answer it requires:

- ♥ A willingness to take an honest look at your relationship—your compatibility, your strengths and weaknesses, and your current ability to make a strong
  decision.

- ♥ A biblical understanding of how God leads in our
  lives.

We will address these topics in the following two chapters. For
some of you these chapters will provide an opportunity to take
an honest look at your relationship and ask some needed questions about whether you are moving in the right direction. For
others they will confirm the decisions you've already made.

NAVIGATING BY
TRUE NORTH
Truths to Chart Your Course

♥ The commitment to *receive* your mate as God's perfect provision for you must be based on faith in God's integrity.

♥ The commitment to leave your parents means cutting the cord of dependence and allegiance.

♥ The commitment to cleave to your mate is an unconditional, irrevocable choice of your will. Marriage is a permanent, sacred covenant, and should not be taken lightly.

♥ The commitment to become one flesh creates a divinely mysterious union—emotional, physical and spiritual transparency—that in God's plan must never precede marriage.

♥ When you build from God's blueprint, *one plus one equals one.*

♥ God must be at the center of your lives and your marriage.

A SPECIAL MESSAGE
on Sexual Purity and Cohabitation

From the world's viewpoint, maintaining sexual purity before marriage seems like cruel and unusual punishment. Many people consider it strange if a couple does not sleep together before they are married.

Many couples today are also following the world's plan in preparing for marriage. More than half of couples getting married today are living together before the wedding ceremony; the world's wisdom holds that this time of cohabitation is a good trial run for the marriage—a test to see if they are truly compatible.[2]

We want to challenge you to commit yourself to following God's plan rather than the world's as you prepare for marriage.

Sexual Purity

The culture portrays sexual intimacy between two unmarried people as casual and as innocuous as holding hands. And it is assumed that sex is a natural part of a serious relationship.

God's Word makes it clear, however, that sex is a gift that is to be enjoyed between a husband and wife (see more in chapter 8). Read the following verses and seek to understand God's perspective:

You shall not commit adultery (Exod. 20:14).

Now flee from youthful lusts and pursue righteousness, faith, love and peace, with those who call on the Lord from a pure heart (2 Tim. 2:22).

Just as He chose us in Him before the foundation of the world, that we should be holy and blameless before Him (Eph. 1:4).

As obedient children, do not be conformed to the former lusts which were yours in ignorance, but like the

Holy One who called you, be holy yourselves also in all your behavior; because it is written, "YOU SHALL BE HOLY, FOR I AM HOLY" (1 Pet. 1:14-16).

Now for this very reason also, applying all diligence, in your faith supply moral excellence, and in your moral excellence knowledge, and in your knowledge, self-control, and in your self-control, perseverance, and in your perseverance, godliness; and in your godliness, brotherly kindness, and in your brotherly kindness, love (2 Pet. 1:5-7).

But immorality or any impurity or greed must not even be named among you, as is proper among saints (Eph. 5:3).

Marriage is to be held in honor among all, and the marriage bed is to be undefiled; for fornicators and adulterers God will judge (Heb. 13:4).

Finally, brethren, whatever is true, whatever is honorable, whatever is right, whatever is pure, whatever is lovely, whatever is of good repute, if there is any excellence and if anything worthy of praise, dwell on these things (Phil. 4:8).

But I want you to be wise in what is good and innocent in what is evil (Rom. 16:19b).

It is easy to know another person sexually. But a marriage relationship requires much more than physical intimacy. There first needs to be spiritual and emotional intimacy to build trust, commitment and communication. Marriage is a lifelong covenant to love and care and nourish.

It's important to remember that God always has our best interests in mind. He designed sexual intercourse to strengthen a bond that He has already made strong—like reinforcing steel rods in concrete.

There are many benefits to staying pure before marriage. By waiting until marriage:

- ☐ You please God.
- ☐ You will be able to develop a much clearer conviction of how God is working in your relationship.
- ☐ You build the trust that is necessary for true intimacy and for lifelong commitment.
- ☐ You develop the godly qualities of patience and self-control.
- ☐ You affirm that you care more for the other person than for yourself.
- ☐ You protect yourself from feelings of guilt and shame.
- ☐ You help protect yourself from the emotional, mental and even physical trauma that can come when you break off a relationship.
- ☐ You have a greater opportunity to develop a stronger emotional and spiritual bond—you can develop healthy communication habits and skills, and discover more about each other than just the physical.
- ☐ You prevent unwanted pregnancy.
- ☐ You maintain a clear conscience before God and man.
- ☐ You increase the anticipation and enjoyment of your wedding night.
- ☐ You experience the blessing of obedience.
- ☐ You maintain a witness to a lost world.
- ☐ You provide yourself with an example to give your children.
- ☐ You avoid bringing reproach on the name of Christ.

Put a checkmark beside the five benefits that strike a chord in your heart. Share these benefits with your fiancé(e) and why you chose them.

Moral Excellence

Sexual purity is especially difficult during the engagement period. You have declared your commitment and you naturally
want to consummate the relationship. You may even feel married at times. Yet what better time to establish your relationship and build trust in one another than by obeying God on
this key point?

It's also important to realize that sexual purity means
much more than avoiding sexual intercourse. Look again at
the verses quoted above. Scripture defines sexual purity as being morally excellent, and moral excellence means *being holy*.
It means avoiding the appearance of evil. It means purity of
thought as well as purity of deed. And it means protecting
each other's innocence from being stained by evil.

Our challenge to you is to do much more than remain abstinent
until your marriage. Our challenge is to be pure.

Answer the following questions individually, then discuss
them with your fiancé(e):

1. What have been your limits and boundaries in the sexual
   area of your relationship until now?

   _____

   _____

   _____

   _____

   _____

   _____

2. What has been your experience in holding to these
   boundaries?

   _____

   _____

   _____

   _____

   _____

   _____

3. Now write a one-sentence definition for moral excellence as it relates to your physical relationship.

_____

_____

_____

_____

_____

Moral excellence in our physical relationship means:

_____

_____

_____

_____

_____

4. Based on your definition, check the boxes that give you the specific boundaries that you believe God wants you to hold to in your physical relationship.

❐ We will not spend the night in the same bed.
❐ We will not be alone after 10:00 p.m.
❐ We will not lay next to each other in any setting.
❐ We will not fondle or pet each other.
❐ We will not give each other massages.
❐ We will not kiss until the wedding ceremony.
❐ We will not do anything that we would be embarrassed to tell Jesus we did.
❐ We will not touch each other anywhere that clothing would normally cover.
❐ Other: _____

As you understand God's desire for your moral purity, pray and ask God to show you if there is anything you need to apologize to your fiancé(e) for and seek forgiveness in this area. If there is, take the time to address it now in prayer with God and with your fiancé(e).

First John 1:9 says that if we confess our sins (agree with God concerning our sin), "He is faithful and righteous to forgive us our sins and to cleanse us from all unrighteousness." You can start right now with a clean slate.

After discussing this with your fiancé(e), it may be appropriate for you both to confess this to your mentor couple and ask them to pray for you, help you set limits and hold you accountable to them.

Cohabitation

A major shift has occurred in our culture during the last 40 years: A growing number of couples are living together before they are married. The U.S. Census Bureau reported that by 2005, nearly 10 million people were living with someone of the opposite sex, up from about 878,000 in 1960. Many of these couples view cohabitation as a trial run to see if marriage would work. As one woman writes, "I couldn't imagine getting hitched to anyone I hadn't taken on a test-spin as a roommate. Conjoin with someone before sharing a bathroom? Not likely!"[3]

The dramatic rise in cohabitation can be traced to several factors: modern attitudes about sex; young adults waiting longer to get married; a growing ignorance of God's biblical plan; a general devaluation of marriage as an institution; and the fear of many individuals of ending up divorced like their parents. To many couples, it makes sense to live together and determine if this relationship will last before making the commitment of marriage. Living together is the normal type of premarriage relationship portrayed in countless movies and television shows. With each new generation of young people, the number of cohabiting couples is expected to rise.

If you are now living with your fiancé(e), we urge you to use this experience of working through *Preparing for Marriage* as an opportunity to give your lives and your future to God and then take steps to ensure that your marriage is the best it can be. Make a commitment to live apart, to abstain from sexual intimacy and to make a clear decision on whether God is calling you together in marriage.

Here is a question to consider: Does living together really give you a good trial run for marriage?

There are many factors at play here. For one thing, while many couples believe that cohabitation simulates a marriage relationship, many researchers and counselors point out that it's actually a false copy of the real thing. Dr. Willard Harley writes:

> I suggest that you consider why couples who live together don't marry. Ask yourself that very question. Why did you choose to live with your boyfriend instead of marrying him?
>
> The answer is that you were not ready to make that commitment to him yet. First, you wanted to see if you still loved him after you cooked meals together, cleaned the apartment together and slept together. In other words, you wanted to see what married life would be like without the commitment of marriage.
>
> But what you don't seem to realize is that you will never know what married life is like *unless* you're married. The commitment of marriage adds a dimension to your relationship that puts everything on its ear. Right now, you are testing each other to see if you are compatible. If either of you slips up, the test is over, and you are out the door. Marriage doesn't work that way. Slip-ups don't end the marriage, they just end the love you have for each other.
>
> What, exactly, is the commitment of marriage? It is an agreement that you will take care of each other for life, regardless of life's ups and downs. You will stick it out together through thick and thin. But the commitment of living together isn't like that at all. It is simply a month-to-month rental agreement.[4]

In other words, living together cannot work as a trial run to determine if you are able to make the commitment of marriage, because that commitment cannot be experienced unless you *are* married. *This commitment is what sets marriage apart from every other relationship.* It changes everything.

Another problem with living together is what researchers call "relationship inertia." Couples grow accustomed to living together, and they decide to get married because that seems like what they should do next. They may give in to pressure from parents, or they may feel they "owe each other" after investing so much of their lives in the relationship. As Dr. Scott Stanley, a professor of Family and Marital Studies at the University of Denver, says, "People who are cohabiting might end up marrying somebody they might not otherwise have married." They are "sliding, not deciding," he says.[5]

A Test of Your Faith

In the end, these decisions—about whether you will engage in sexual relations before marriage and whether you will live together—reveal much about what you believe. Are you willing to believe what God's Word says about building the type of relationship that will last a lifetime? Are you willing to believe in His plan for marriage? Are you willing to follow Him? Are you willing to believe He knows what is best for you and your future?

And if you and your fiancé(e) are not willing to put your faith in God on issues like these, why do you think you are ready for marriage?

Notes

1. Clifford L. and Joyce J. Penner, *The Gift of Sex* (Nashville, TN: W Publishing Group, 2003), p. 22.

2. In the September 2002 issue of *Research on Today's Issues,* the National Institute of Child Health and Human Development reported that 54 percent of all first marriages between 1990 and 1994 failed. All indications have shown that this percentage has continued to increase since that time; in the 2007 American Community Survey, the U.S. Census Bureau reported there are more than 5.5 million opposite-sex unmarried households—more than 11 million people.

3. Nancy Wartik, "The Perils of Playing House," *Psychology Today*, July 1, 2005.

4. Dr. Willard Harley, "Living Together Before Marriage," http://www.marriage builders.com/graphic/mbi5025_qa.html.

5. Dr. Scott Stanley, quoted in "Cohabitation Is Replacing Dating," *USA Today*, July 17, 2005. http://usatoday.com/life/lifestyle/2005-07-17-cohabitation_x.htm.

Couple's Project

 GET REAL

Interact as a couple on the following activities.

1. Spend a few minutes going through "Get the Picture" and "Get the Truth," sharing and discussing your answers to the different questions. Be sure to ask your fiancé(e) to explain the answers.

2. Answer the following two questions individually, and then share your answers with each other:

   a. As you consider leaving your parents, which of the two "cords"—the cord of dependence and the cord of allegiance—will be the most difficult for you to sever?

   _____
   _____
   _____
   _____

   b. Which of the two cords mentioned above will be the most difficult for your fiancé(e) to sever?

   _____
   _____
   _____

3. Discuss with your fiancé(e) ways in which you can honor each set of parents as you clearly cut the cords of dependency and allegiance.

   _____

   _____

   _____

4. What have been your feelings about divorce up to this point? How have those feelings been influenced by your own family history?

   _____

   _____

   _____

   _____

5. Indicate whether you agree or disagree with the following statement, and why: "Jesus Christ is at the center of my life."

   _____

   _____

   _____

   _____

6. Indicate whether you agree or disagree with the following statement, and why: "Our relationship has a solid foundation with Christ at the center."

   _____

   _____

   _____

   _____

7. Conclude this section by writing a brief paragraph describing the place you want God to take in your marriage.

   _____

   _____

   _____

   _____

GET TO THE HEART
of Your Marriage

One of the best ways to learn to pray more effectively is to write out your prayers. Take a few moments and write down a two- or three-sentence prayer expressing your desire to build your marriage according to God's plan.

Here is a suggested prayer to help you get started:

Dear God,
It is our desire to build a marriage that honors You, the creator of marriage. To do that we need to both build according to Your plan. Today, we pledge to You that Your plans of receiving, leaving, cleaving and becoming one flesh will be the blueprint for our marriage. In Christ's name, amen.

_____
_____
_____
_____
_____
_____

After you have both jotted down a short prayer, kneel side by side if you are able to, and together pray to God.

 # GET DEEPER

Here are two special optional assignments for those who want to go deeper.

1. Read chapter 12 in *Staying Close*, by Dennis Rainey.

2. For further reading on honoring your parents, read *The Best You Can Give Your Parents*, by Dennis Rainey with David Boehi.

SPECIAL QUESTIONS
for Those Who Were Previously Married

1. Did you find it difficult to receive your mate in your first marriage? In what ways?

_____

_____

_____

_____

2. Did you find it difficult to leave your parents? Why?

_____

_____

_____

_____

3. Did you begin the marriage with a commitment to stay married for life? As you look back now, what eroded that commitment?

_____

_____

_____

_____

4. What unique challenges will you face in each of the following areas in a new marriage?

Receive:

_____

_____

_____

Leave:

_____

_____

_____

Cleave:

_____
_____
_____
_____

Become one flesh:

_____
_____
_____
_____

5. If your fiancé(e) has children, how does this affect your ability to receive him or her as God's gift to you?

_____
_____
_____
_____

6. How will you relate to your previous in-laws? What kind of relationship will your children have with them?

_____
_____
_____
_____

Bonus

Purity Covenant

1. Take the Purity Covenant and place it before you. Read through the sections one at a time.

2. After you have read through all three passages and the commitments, sign and date the Covenant.

3. If they are not with you as you read and sign, have your mentor couple/pastor/counselor sign the Purity Covenant at your next meeting. They will ask you if you are honoring your covenant before signing.

Purity Covenant

Biblical Standard

First Thessalonians 4:3-8: "For this is the will of God, your sanctification; that is, that you abstain from sexual immorality; that each of you know how to possess his own vessel in sanctification and honor, not in lustful passion, like the Gentiles who do not know God; and that no man transgress and defraud his brother in the matter because the Lord is the avenger in all these things, just as we also told you before and solemnly warned you. For God has not called us for the purpose of impurity, but in sanctification. So, he who rejects this is not rejecting man but the God who gives His Holy Spirit to you."

In obedience to God's command, I promise to protect your sexual purity from this day until our wedding night.

Biblical Standard
First Corinthians 6:18-20: "Flee immorality. Every other sin that a man commits is outside the body, but the immoral man sins against his own body. Or do you not know that your body is a temple of the Holy Spirit who is in you, whom you have from God, and that you are not your own? For you have been bought with a price: therefore glorify God in your body."

Because I respect and honor you, I commit to building up the inner person of your heart rather than violating you.

Biblical Standard
Acts 24:16: "In view of this, I also do my best to maintain always a blameless conscience both before God and before men."

I pledge to show my love for you in ways that allow both of us to maintain a clear conscience before God and each other.

THIS IS MY PROMISE OF PURITY

_____ Date _____

_____ Date _____

Witnessed/affirmed

_____ Date _____

part three

making the decision

Elections are a good deal like marriages. There's no accounting for anyone's taste. Every time we see a bridegroom we wonder why she ever picked him, and it's the same with public officials.

WILL ROGERS

What you are as a single person, you will be as a married person, only to a greater degree. Any negative character trait will be intensified in a marriage relationship, because you will feel free to let your guard down—that person has committed himself to you and you no longer have to worry about scaring him off.

JOSH MCDOWELL

Chapter 3

Evaluating Your Relationship

 TRUE NORTH

*To make a good decision about marriage,
it's important to appraise your fiancé(e) and
your relationship with a sound mind.*

 GET THE PICTURE

No other human relationship will play a more important role
in shaping your life than your relationship with your spouse.
Yet many people make the crucial decisions about marriage
when their minds are clouded with such powerful emotions
that they find it difficult to think straight. They are so caught
up in the whirlwind of romance that they fail to work out some
crucial issues before they commit their lives to each other.

This chapter is designed to help you evaluate your relationship and think through some of these important issues.
Whether you and your fiancé(e) are already engaged or just seriously contemplating marriage, working through this material
will force you to ask some challenging questions about your relationship. Specifically, here's what we want to help you do:

* Evaluate your compatibility.
* Eliminate any encumbrance that hinders you from
  thinking clearly about the relationship.

Yes, this process may seem unromantic. But if your goal is to build a true oneness marriage—an intimate relationship that is all that God intended—then this decision needs to be made with your mind and will as well as your emotions.

If you have already decided to marry, then allow this section to confirm your direction. Stay open to what God wants for you. Ask the difficult questions. Have the courage to be honest.

If you have not yet decided, then allow this material to help guide you. As you work through the process, you can be confident that your decision is informed, balanced and biblical.

Get the Truth

When two people are "compatible," they are able to live together in harmony. Their personalities may be totally different, and their interests may not match. But they have learned to live together in spite of those differences because of a few factors that do match.

Relational Compatibility

As your relationship grows more serious, it's important to examine your everyday relationship—your relational skills, the quality of your friendship and the way your two personalities mesh.

If you are meeting with a counselor or mentor, you may already have completed some type of personality or temperament survey. Tests such as the Taylor-Johnson Temperament Analysis, the PREPARE test or the Myers-Briggs Type Indicator will give you invaluable information to see how well you and your fiancé(e) mesh. If you are not planning to complete one of these tests, this exercise will help provide a basic understanding of how well you fit together.

1. Complete the chart below. For each choice (e.g., Disciplined versus Impulsive), put an X on the number that

best describes you and a circle around the number that best describes your fiancé(e). For example: If you think that you are more disciplined than impulsive, you would put an X on the left side of the line between those two choices. If you think that your fiancé(e) is very impulsive, you'd put an O on the far right side of that line.

Disciplined	1	2	3	4	5	6	7	8	9	10	Impulsive
Stubborn	1	2	3	4	5	6	7	8	9	10	Humble
Aggressive/ assertive	1	2	3	4	5	6	7	8	9	10	Compliant/ passive
Task-oriented	1	2	3	4	5	6	7	8	9	10	People-oriented
Pessimistic	1	2	3	4	5	6	7	8	9	10	Optimistic
Fast-paced	1	2	3	4	5	6	7	8	9	10	Slow-paced
Socially active	1	2	3	4	5	6	7	8	9	10	Withdrawn
Sympathetic	1	2	3	4	5	6	7	8	9	10	Insensitive
Decisive	1	2	3	4	5	6	7	8	9	10	Indecisive
Tense	1	2	3	4	5	6	7	8	9	10	Relaxed
Emotionally open	1	2	3	4	5	6	7	8	9	10	Emotionally closed
Good self-image	1	2	3	4	5	6	7	8	9	10	Poor self-image
Critical	1	2	3	4	5	6	7	8	9	10	Patient
Idealistic	1	2	3	4	5	6	7	8	9	10	Realistic
Controlling	1	2	3	4	5	6	7	8	9	10	Permissive
Affectionate	1	2	3	4	5	6	7	8	9	10	Reserved
Verbal	1	2	3	4	5	6	7	8	9	10	Quiet
Responsible	1	2	3	4	5	6	7	8	9	10	Irresponsible

2. In what areas do you and your fiancé(e) balance each other?

_____

_____

_____

_____

_____

3. How have you seen your differences benefit your relationship?

_____

_____

_____

_____

_____

4. What differences have caused friction and conflict in your relationship?

_____

_____

_____

_____

_____

5. How often do you experience conflict? How do you work out conflict?

_____

_____

_____

_____

6. How do your friends and family feel about your relationship? Do they feel that you "fit" together?

_____

_____

_____

_____

7. Does anything here cause you to doubt whether you should continue the relationship?

_____

_____

_____

_____

A WORD ABOUT COMPATIBILITY AND COMMITMENT

There is no black-and-white formula for evaluating all these factors. The key is how they play out in your relationship, and how you feel about them. For example, you may be concerned about your differences in the way you relate to other people. Yet you may find that your differences complement each other in unique ways.

God often seems to bring together two people who are different in many ways. For example, a fast-paced wife ends up marrying a slower-paced husband. A people-oriented husband chooses a task-oriented wife.

Identifying your similarities and differences in these areas is only the first step toward determining compatibility. You also need to address how your differences may make you stronger as a team, and how your commitment could compensate for your differences.

Spiritual Compatibility
Because marriage is a spiritual relationship, your spiritual compatibility will influence the quality of your relationship more than any other factor. There are two topics to consider here:

Are Both of You Christians?
In 2 Corinthians 6:14-15, Paul writes:

> Do not be bound together with unbelievers; for what partnership have righteousness and lawlessness, or what fellowship has light with darkness? Or what harmony has Christ with Belial [Satan], or what has a believer in common with an unbeliever?

This passage warns that a Christian should not enter a partnership with an unbeliever because it will be a relationship built on opposing values and goals. Building relationships on Christian values, trust and love is essential in the Christian life, especially in the most intimate of all human relationships—marriage. God created marriage, and its greatest fulfillment and enjoyment can only be found when both husband and wife have a growing relationship with Him.

When Christians marry nonbelievers, they usually experience a growing frustration after marriage:

- ♥ They are unable to discuss the most precious, intimate part of their lives with their spouses.
- ♥ They have conflicting goals and expectations.
- ♥ They clash over the values they teach their children.
- ♥ The have differing circles of friends.
- ♥ They have difficulty communicating and resolving conflict.

If one of you has received Christ as Lord and Savior, but the other has not, we strongly recommend that you either put your relationship on hold or end it altogether. Don't allow yourself to adopt a missionary mindset, where you think you can lead your fiancé(e) to Christ, either before or after marriage. If your fiancé(e) is unwilling to repent and change now, don't expect it to happen after you marry.

Second, if neither of you has received Christ, we recommend that you put off any wedding plans so you can focus on learning more about a relationship with Him. Give yourselves time to talk with Christian friends, or your pastor, and come to a solid decision about where you stand with God.

Do You Both Share the Same Commitment to Spiritual Growth and to Serving God?
Many Christians know they should not marry a nonbeliever. Unfortunately, they go no further in evaluating their spiritual compatibility.

First John 2:15 tells us, "Do not love the world nor the things in the world. If any one loves the world, the love of the Father is not in him." You may both have received Christ, but if one of you is more focused on loving the world rather than loving God, you will experience many of the same conflicts as a believer and nonbeliever. Your goals and values will differ. Your lives will head in different directions.

If you are both growing in Christ, however, you will experience a special joy and teamwork in your marriage. Running coaches usually encourage their long-distance runners to train in groups rather than as individuals. In a group, runners encourage and push each other to ignore their weariness and pain. In fact, a runner may run faster in a group than he would by himself, yet feel less fatigued. In the same way, two people who share the same commitment to God can encourage and help each other to keep their eyes on Christ as they "run with endurance" (see Heb. 12:1).

To evaluate this area of your spiritual compatibility, begin by asking yourself questions such as:

- Do both of us share the same desire to know and please God?
- Do I have any sense that one of us is putting on a façade of spiritual commitment?
- Do our actions back up our words?
- Do we both consistently display a desire to obey God in all things?
- What priority does each of us place on ministering to other people?
- Are we both willing to follow God's direction?

If you cannot shake a suspicion that you and your fiancé(e) are on different wavelengths in your spiritual compatibility, we strongly advise you, again, to postpone any wedding plans. If not, you will likely experience a distressing level of isolation in your marriage.

8. How would you rate your spiritual compatibility at this time?

_____

_____

_____

_____

9. What changes would need to occur in you to increase your spiritual compatibility?

_____

_____

_____

_____

_____

10. What changes do you think would need to occur in your fiancé(e) to increase your spiritual compatibility?

_____

_____

_____

_____

_____

Seeing Through the Fog

Have you ever tried to drive in a dense fog? It's an eerie feeling. All you can see is the area directly in front of you. Buildings and other vehicles seem like ghosts. Sounds are muted.

It's also dangerous, especially if you proceed too fast. And yet many couples can be compared to drivers speeding at 70 miles per hour through a dense fog, supremely confident that they are safe yet unable to see anything that lies more than 30 feet ahead. Where once these couples saw clearly, now their minds are clouded by conflicting thoughts and emotions, yet they press on in the relationship without slowing down.

We have identified seven factors that can easily hinder a couple in a serious relationship from seeing clearly.

Idealistic Thinking

In the excitement of the relationship, everything seems wonderful. You may have a difficult time discerning any faults in this person. If you do see problems, you are confident that these will go away after you are married.

Loneliness

You're tired of living on your own, and you long for the companionship of marriage. Your friends are all getting married, and you wonder if something is wrong with you. You aren't getting any younger, and, if you're a woman, you may feel the inevitable ticking of your biological clock.

Sexual Involvement

Premarital sexual involvement can prevent you from clearly evaluating other aspects of the relationship. It also can produce guilt or shame that lingers on into marriage.

Spiritual Immaturity

One or both of you may be in a period of rebellion, walking out of fellowship with God. This may be the temporary result of unconfessed sin in your life, or it may be a long-term pattern going back many years. Or you may sincerely desire to grow in your relationship with Christ, but you don't know how. You have no sense of how God may be leading in the relationship because you have no idea how to discern His voice.

Wedding Preparations

If you're already engaged and moving swiftly toward your wedding date, you've already seen that planning a wedding is like riding a runaway train. The faster you go, the harder it is to stop. So if you develop serious doubts about the relationship, the thought of canceling or postponing a wedding feels unthinkable.

The factors we've just discussed may lead you to make an unwise or premature commitment to your fiancé(e). Or they may make it difficult to end an unwise relationship. The final two, however, may *prevent* you from making a commitment:

Fear of Failure
You are troubled by thoughts of not living up to the expectations of your fiancé(e), your peers, your family or yourself. You feel that you will be unable to make a marriage work. Perhaps your parents' marriage ended in divorce, and you don't want that to happen to you.

Fear of Commitment
While you long for the benefits of marriage, you feel a deep, profound, grave sense of dread when you contemplate making a lifelong commitment to another person. You realize that if someone better comes along, you are stuck. You are paralyzed to move ahead.

11. Look over this list of seven relational fog producers. Which of these are issues in your relationship?

_____

_____

_____

12. If you have some serious concerns, are you willing to take the time you need to ensure that you make a good decision about marriage? Why or why not?

_____

_____

_____

_____

If you have concerns, be sure to discuss them with a counselor, pastor or mentor.

Heeding Relational Red Flags

Any relationship will have its difficulties, but sometimes those problems are indicators of deep-rooted problems that, if not addressed quickly, will poison your marriage. If any of the following red flags—caution signs—exist in your relationship, we recommend that you talk about the situation as soon as possible with a pastor, counselor or mentor.

Part of this list was adapted by permission from Bob Phillips, author of *How Can I Be Sure: A Pre-Marriage Inventory*.[1]

- You have a general uneasy feeling that something is wrong in your relationship.

- You find yourself arguing often with your fiancé(e).

- Your fiancé(e) seems irrationally angry and jealous whenever you interact with someone of the opposite sex.

- You avoid discussing certain subjects because you're afraid of your fiancé(e)'s reaction.

- Your fiancé(e) finds it extremely difficult to express emotions, or is prone to extreme emotions (such as out-of-control anger or exaggerated fear). Or he/she swings back and forth between emotional extremes (such as being very happy one minute, then suddenly exhibiting extreme sadness the next).

- Your fiancé(e) displays controlling behavior. This means more than a desire to be in charge—it means your fiancé(e) seems to want to control every aspect of your life: your appearance, your lifestyle, your interactions with friends or family, and so on. Your fiancé(e) seems to manipulate you into doing what he or she wants.

- You are continuing the relationship because of fear—of hurting your fiancé(e), or of what he or she might do if you ended the relationship.

- Your fiancé(e) does not treat you with respect. He or she constantly criticizes you or talks sarcastically to you, even in public.

- Your fiancé(e) is unable to hold down a job, doesn't take personal responsibility for losing a job, or frequently borrows money from you or from friends.

- Your fiancé(e) often talks about aches and pains, and you suspect some of these are imagined. He or she goes from doctor to doctor until finding someone who will agree that there is some type of illness.

- Your fiancé(e) is unable to resolve conflict. He or she cannot deal with constructive criticism, or never admits a mistake, or never asks for forgiveness.

- Your fiancé(e) is overly dependant on parents for finances, decision-making or emotional security.

- Your fiancé(e) is consistently dishonest and tries to keep you from learning about certain aspects of his or her life.

- Your fiancé(e) does not appear to recognize right from wrong, and rationalizes questionable behavior.

- Your fiancé(e) consistently avoids responsibility.

- Your fiancé(e) exhibits patterns of physical, emotional or sexual abuse toward you or others.

- Your fiancé(e) displays signs of drug or alcohol abuse: unexplained absences of missed dates, frequent car accidents, the smell of alcohol or strong odor of mouthwash, erratic behavior or emotional swings, physical signs such as red eyes, unkempt look, unexplained nervousness, and so on.

- Your fiancé(e) has displayed a sudden, dramatic change in lifestyle after you began dating. (He or she may be changing just to win you and will revert back to old habits after marriage.)

- Your fiancé(e) has trouble controlling anger. He or she uses anger as a weapon or as a means of winning arguments.

- You have a difficult time trusting your fiancé(e)—to fulfill responsibilities, to be truthful, to help in times of need, to make ethical decisions, and so on.

- Your fiancé(e) has a history of multiple serious relationships that have failed—a pattern of knowing how to begin a relationship but not knowing how to keep one growing.

Look over this list. Do any of these red flags apply to your relationship? If so, we recommend you talk about the situation as soon as possible with a pastor, counselor or mentor.

SPECIAL WARNING

If any of these red flags are present in your relationship and you are engaging in sexual intercourse, it is imperative that you terminate the physical intimacy immediately. As we've already discussed, God has your welfare in mind when He forbids sexual connection before marriage. The premature bond this type of intimacy creates will make it extremely difficult for you to make needed changes in your relationship or to break it off.

Note

1. Bob Phillips, *How Can I Be Sure: A Pre-Marriage Inventory* (Eugene, OR: Harvest House Publishers, 1978).

Remember, just as the turning of a steering wheel of an automobile
does not alter its direction unless it is moving, so God cannot direct our
lives unless we are moving for Him.

BILL BRIGHT

Chapter 4

A Decision-Making Guide

 TRUE NORTH

You won't miss God's will for your life if you walk closely with Him.

It's as inevitable as night following day. As their relationship grows more serious, two people begin asking the question, "Is God leading us together?" It's a key question, because receiving each other as God's provision (see chapter 2) requires a conviction that He has brought you together.

 GET THE PICTURE

Many Christians find it difficult to explain how they determine God's will for important decisions in their lives. Ask one hundred Christians, "How do you know God's will?" and you will receive so many different answers that you will wonder if they read the same Bible.

We asked a number of married couples, "How did you determine whether God was calling you to be married?" Here are some of their answers:

> "From the moment I saw her I knew she was special. We used to look into each other's eyes and ask each other if we were really supposed to be together, and we

literally would get this real tingly feeling, both of us together at the same time. It's hard to explain. It gave chills through my whole body."

"I knew she would be good for me. Her personality really complements mine. The things that I am weak in, she is strong in. She is a godly woman and I just felt like she was the one for me, I guess. I can't point to anything concrete besides the fact that we spent time praying about it, but at a certain point the timing was just right, and we were just relying on God's timing. And I felt like I didn't have a red light from God. He didn't stop me."

"We hit it off as such close friends. I felt like I had known her for my whole life. Also, she was a Christian, and I wanted to marry someone who believed as I did. So I knew it was God's will. I had a feeling of peace about it."

As you can see, Christians have many different ideas about how to know God's will. The problem is that sometimes we receive misinformation, especially on the subject of choosing a mate. For example, many Christians believe they will have a "feeling of peace" if they are following God. Yet, sometimes, following God's leading may lead to great fear and anxiety, like going to someone you've hurt to apologize and seek forgiveness. Our feelings and emotions are so fickle that to depend on them as an indicator of God's will is like deciding to go to work each day based on the weather.

Another common belief is, "God will do something to keep me from making a mistake in choosing a marriage partner." According to this theory, perhaps God will give us a visible sign from heaven or cause us to have an auto accident if we're about to head in the wrong direction. The reality, however, is that it's easy to look for God's voice in the wrong places, especially if we are not accustomed to listening to His Spirit within our hearts.

On the other end of the spectrum is the belief that, apart from what God specifically states in Scripture to do or not to do, we are on our own. Therefore, it doesn't matter whom you marry, as long as the two of you are compatible and you're not disobeying Scripture. However, this philosophy often limits the ministry of the Holy Spirit. The Spirit not only speaks to us through the Word of God but also influences us through other means (though never in contradiction with the Word). The Bible clearly states that God leads in the lives of individuals; the Holy Spirit not only teaches, but also guides.

Going through this decision-making process is one of the most important steps you can take to ensure a oneness marriage:

1. It will help you determine how God is leading in your relationship.
2. It will formally seal the decision you have made to marry.
3. It will give you a landmark to look back on during times of doubt and fear.
4. It is a healthy process for a couple to work through regardless of whether you are engaged or not, because it will ground you in the Word of God and encourage you to keep growing in your relationship with Him.

GET THE TRUTH

If you are deciding whether to become engaged, this chapter will help you learn how to discern God's will. As you read through it, do not feel pressured to make the decision now. This guide provides a biblical framework for making the decision—when you believe it is time to make it.

If you already are engaged, this guide will help you think through some critical issues to ensure that you did not overlook anything in your decision. You may find your decision confirmed or challenged in some areas. Of all the decisions you will make in life, this is one that you will want to expose to the rigors of added scrutiny. Don't be afraid to test your decision by making this guide book a "decision review."

Components of a Biblical Decision

Picture the framework of a biblical decision as a wheel with four spokes. Each part of the wheel represents a necessary component in a biblical decision:

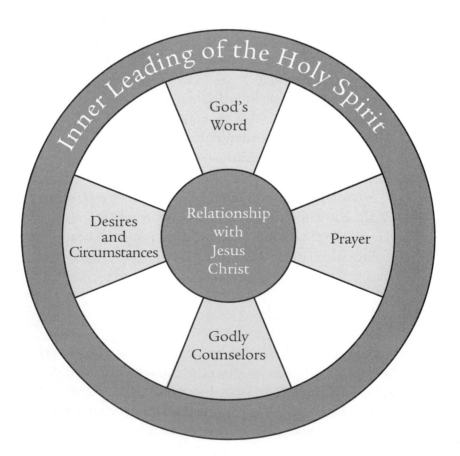

Hub of the Wheel: Your Relationship with Jesus Christ

It is in knowing Him, loving Him, obeying Him, talking with Him, seeking Him—in other words, *relating* to Him—that we come to know His will.

In the Gospel of John, Jesus describes Himself as a shepherd who cares for His sheep: "I am the good shepherd, and I know My own, and My own know Me. . . . My sheep hear My voice, and I know them, and they follow Me" (John 10:14,27).

As you develop an intimate relationship with Christ, you will come to know His voice—how He speaks to you, how He leads in your life. And the more you know God, the more you are willing to trust Him with your life.

First Spoke of the Wheel: God's Word

By spending time reading the Bible, you allow God to speak to you directly. In some cases, God's Word will address areas of your relationship that are not pleasing to Him. And it will provide wisdom and guidance as you make your decision.

Psalm 119:105 states, "Your word is a lamp to my feet and a light to my path." As we've seen, God's Word provides guidelines for a marriage relationship.

Second Spoke: Prayer

James 1:5 says, "But if any of you lacks wisdom, let him ask of God, who gives to all generously and without reproach, and it will be given to him." We need to ask God for wisdom. In other words, we need to pray.

These first two spokes, God's Word and prayer, are the primary ways that the Holy Spirit directs your decision. Through asking (prayer) and seeking (time in God's Word) the Holy Spirit guides.

Third Spoke: Godly Counselors

As Proverbs 19:20 says, "Listen to counsel and accept discipline, that you may be wise the rest of your days." By consulting with mature, godly friends or family members—or with a premarriage counselor—you benefit from their experience and perspective. Someone who has traveled further down the road you are walking can provide valuable insight.

Additionally, because they are not so close to the details, they can offer a "big picture" perspective. They may be able to spot strengths and weaknesses in your relationship much quicker than you. They also may be able to help you sort through your emotions to make a clear decision. It is important that you seek out a godly counselor who will tell you what you need to hear, not someone who tells you what you want to hear.

Final Spoke: Desires and Circumstances

Often, in our efforts to find God's will, we deny our own personal preferences and desires. Philippians 2:13 reads, "For it is God who is at work in you, both to will and to work for His good pleasure." You see, God does place desires within us for our good. Assuming that you are growing in your relationship with the Lord and seeking His will, recognizing your desires can be an important part of the process. For example, do you *want* to be married at this point in your life? Do you *want* to marry *this* particular person? Is there anything about this person that you particularly dislike?

In addition, as you look at your relationship, ask yourself whether events and circumstances seem to confirm that it's heading in the right direction.

Rim of the Wheel: Inner Leading of the Holy Spirit

As you spend time with God, pray, seek godly counsel, consider your compatibility, evaluate your desires and circumstances, and wholeheartedly submit to God, the Holy Spirit will guide you. The Scriptures tell us the Holy Spirit guides (see John 16:13) and teaches us (see John 14:26), and acts as our Helper (see John 14:16,26). The Greek word often used in the New Testament to describe the Spirit, *Parakletos,* means "one called to the side of another—with a view to providing help."

God may not speak in an audible voice to Christians today as He did in the Old Testament, and as He did through His Son, Jesus Christ. But He still speaks to our hearts.

Many Christians, as they seek God's will, look for some sort of miraculous sign. They want God to speak to them as He did to Moses—through a burning bush, or a billboard that says, "Marry her!! This is My will for you!" Instead, God gave us His Spirit to live within us and provide guidance, counsel and enlightenment. Our job is to stay close to God, to keep in step with the Spirit (see Gal. 5:25), to listen and obey and yield to His leading.

The Holy Spirit uses three primary means of conveying the will of God.

1. *He speaks through His Word, the Bible.* You may be reading a passage from Scripture for perhaps the twentieth time, but this time it becomes clearer than ever before, and you realize it applies to a problem you're facing. The Spirit serves as our Teacher as we pore through God's Word.

2. *He reveals how God is working.* In their outstanding workbook *Experiencing God*, Henry T. Blackaby and Claude V. King explain that, in Scripture, God's usual pattern is to reveal to individuals what He is doing and then invite them to join Him in this work. Sometimes this experience feels like scales falling from your eyes. You look at your circumstances, or your relationship, and suddenly you see it in a different perspective. You look back over the months and suddenly see the hand of God bringing you together—or perhaps you realize that He has worked in your heart in such a way that you know this relationship is not His will. In whatever situation, you have a definite sense that God has worked in your life.

3. *He speaks through the development of inner convictions.* As you look at your circumstances, you see them in a

new light that clarifies what you need to do. You are talking with a neighbor, and suddenly you sense an unmistakable impression that you should tell her about what Christ means to you.

A conviction from the Holy Spirit grows and matures over time. As you spend time with God, in hours of prayer and Bible study, you know what He desires in your life. For example:

- A middle-aged executive is disillusioned and unfulfilled in his career, and he has a growing desire to be directly involved in helping others know Christ. After a few months, he realizes that God has given him the conviction to work in a full-time Christian ministry.

- Both parents of three young children work and are able to afford a large, beautiful home as a result. Over time, however, they become concerned about the high number of hours they devote to their careers. They realize that God has put it on their hearts to make their children a greater priority in their lives, so they make three decisions: The husband reduces the number of hours he works each week; the wife decides to work part-time out of her home; and they reduce their monthly house payment by moving into a smaller home.

In the same way, God can give you a conviction about whether He wants you to marry. However, the Holy Spirit's internal guidance must always be consistent with His own character and ministry. That means that three things will always be true of His leading:

- It will glorify Christ.
- It will promote holiness.
- It will be consistent with God's Word.

How Does Your Wheel Look?

As you evaluate your own decision-making process for making your decision about whether to be married, what does your wheel look like? Do you have the right "hub" at the center? Are all the spokes connected to the hub and rim? Are any of the spokes missing or shorter than they need to be?

Beside each question below, answer yes, no, or put a "?" if you are uncertain.

_____ Is Christ the center of your life?

_____ Are you growing in spiritual maturity?

_____ Are you consistently praying and spending time in God's Word?

_____ Have you opened your relationship to the scrutiny of godly counselors?

_____ Have you weighed your desires?

_____ Have you evaluated your circumstances?

Finally:

_____ As you look at all these factors, is the Holy Spirit leading you in a specific direction?

If you and your fiancé(e) can answer yes to all of these questions, you can be confident that you are moving in the right direction. If you cannot answer yes to each question, you need to take the time to address each issue.

Couple's Project

Once you understand the framework of a biblical decision, it's time to work through a process to make your decision.

> ♥ Will I receive this person as God's provision for me?
> ♥ Do I choose to commit myself to this person's good for the rest of my life?

To work through the following process, you'll need to set aside a few hours and find a secluded spot where you can be alone without distractions or interruptions. After you and your fiancé(e) complete the following section individually, meet to discuss your answers.

Step One: Spend Time Alone with God

Begin by spending time praising God for who He is. You might want to take a book of Christian songs and hymns, or read through some psalms. Force yourself to take your mind off anything else in your life. You may find that it takes one or two hours just to relax and focus on God.

Then, make sure you are in fellowship with God by acknowledging any unconfessed sin. As Psalm 66:18 says, "If I regard wickedness in my heart, the Lord will not hear."

Step Two: Declare Your Willingness to Follow God's Will

Many Christians never sense God's will in their lives because they have not taken this crucial step. Follow the advice of the great saint George Müller, who wrote about the process he followed in determining God's will:

> I seek at the beginning to get my heart into such a state that it has no will of its own in regard to a given matter. Nine-tenths of the trouble with people generally is just here. Nine-tenths of the difficulties are overcome when our hearts are ready to do the Lord's will, whatever it may be. When one is truly in this state, it is usually but a little way to the knowledge of what His will is.[1]

Step Three: Make an Honest Evaluation of Your Relationship

Perhaps the most common cause of divorce today is "irreconcilable differences." Two people who entered marriage with stars in their eyes find that, after a few years of trying, they just cannot get along anymore.

The tragedy is that many of these marriages would never have occurred if the couple had been honest about their relationship before they made such a binding commitment. Their emotions were so strong, their desire to marry so overpowering, that they failed to look deeply at questions of character, personality and background.

Look back over your answers to questions in the previous chapter on "Evaluating Your Relationship" and then answer the following questions:

1. How would you rate your relational compatibility?

_____

_____

_____

2. How would you rate your spiritual compatibility?

_____

_____

_____

_____

3. Are you confident that you are able to make a clear decision about your relationship?

_____

_____

_____

_____

_____

4. Are there any issues (see the list of relational red flags) that greatly concern you and cause you to question whether you could spend the rest of your life with your fiancé(e)?

_____

_____

_____

_____

_____

5. What are friends, family members and godly counselors saying about your relationship?

_____

_____

_____

_____

6. Do your desires and the circumstances of your relationship confirm that you are headed in the right direction?

_____

_____

_____

_____

Step Four: Consider Whether This Person Is God's Provision for You

7. Write five reasons why you think this is the right person for you to marry. To help you, consider your responses throughout this workbook, the feedback you've received from godly counselors and the impressions you've received from the Holy Spirit.

    a. _____

    b. _____

    c. _____

    d. _____

    e. _____

8. Now write five reasons why you think this is the right time to marry.

    a. _____

    b. _____

    c. _____

    d. _____

    e. _____

9. Write a one-sentence statement why you believe you are ready to receive this person as God's provision for you:

    _____

    _____

    _____

If you are troubled by fears or doubts: Write them down in a list. Honestly evaluate each one by asking yourself two questions:

- ♥ Is this doubt the result of legitimate questions in my mind?
- ♥ Does it demonstrate any lack of trust in God?

Plan a time to talk these over with your potential fiancé(e). Keep these questions in mind as you discuss your doubts.

- Did he (or she) receive or resist my concerns?
- Is he (or she) open to correcting these relationship problems?
- Is he (or she) willing and able to give and ask for forgiveness?

Step Five: Make a Decision and Act on It by Faith

Once you decide how God is leading in your relationship, your responsibility is to *obey by faith*.

If you decide to get engaged, move forward with confidence. If doubts arise, discuss them openly and honestly. Ask God to continue to confirm your decision over the weeks and months ahead.

If you decide not to get engaged, move forward with confidence. Though this choice entails incredible emotional heartache, you can act by faith, knowing that you made the decision through a biblical framework.

- Ask God to help you end the relationship in a way that is honoring to Him. Show dignity, respect, kindness and honor toward the other person.

- Make a clean break. We strongly suggest that there be no communication for six months. It will be wise to make yourself accountable to godly counsel to hold you to this.

- If, after that time, you think God may be leading you back together, you should seek wise counsel before reestablishing contact.

Remember, God's will is not something that is lost that you need to find. It is not something that He is keeping from you, leaking out hints along the way, keeping you guessing so that you are never quite sure what to do.

On the contrary, God's will is clearly revealed in His Word. He has given you the Holy Spirit to guide you in His Word, to give you understanding and insight. The most important thing you can do in determining God's will is to walk closely with Him, cultivating and developing your relationship with Him moment by moment.

Note

1. George Müller, *Answers to Prayer,* compiled by A.E.C. Brooks (Chicago, IL: Moody Publishers, 2007).

part four

building
oneness

*In an era of increasingly fragile marriages, a couple's ability
to communicate is the single most important contributor
to a stable and satisfying marriage.*

GALLUP POLL REPORT

Chapter 5

Authentic Communication

 TRUE NORTH

The extent to which you can "listen to understand" and "express to be understood" will help determine the level of intimacy and oneness you will experience in your marriage.

It has been said that communication is to a relationship what blood is to the human body. Communication nourishes and sustains a relationship. Remove it, and you no longer have a relationship.

Perhaps that is why, whenever FamilyLife surveys couples attending our Weekend to Remember™ marriage conferences, so many people ask for help about communication and conflict:

- ♥ "How can I express my feelings without feeling selfish?"
- ♥ "I always seem to say the wrong thing to hurt my husband's feelings. How do I prevent this?"
- ♥ "How can we change the patterns of our marriage into a deeper level of intimacy?"
- ♥ "How can we communicate without putting each other on the defensive?"
- ♥ "Why do we argue so much?"
- ♥ "How can I overcome this inability to express my feelings to my spouse, on a permanent and regular basis?"

No doubt, your communication as a couple may feel quite gratifying. Most couples in the process of premarital counseling find that one of the joys of their relationship is that they can (and do) "talk about everything."

However, while your word count may be high, your level of *real communication* may actually be lower than you think. Authentic communication is much more than just talking. It is understanding and being understood; identifying a tone of voice; detecting nonverbal cues; responding appropriately to offense; resolving conflicts; knowing what to say, when to say it and how to say it; experiencing the risks and rewards of knowing and being known; and much more.

As you learned in the first two chapters, marriage is built upon a foundation of a relationship with God. As you establish this spiritual foundation as a couple, it is essential that you see the importance of communication in your relationship.

GET THE PICTURE

Read this case study and then answer the following questions.

Case Study: Eric and Amanda's Communication Problems

"She makes me so mad I could scream."

Eric was enjoying a day of fishing with Scott, an older friend at work. Their relationship had developed to the point that Eric looked forward to the conversation as much as the fishing.

This morning, Eric was frustrated about the conflict he and Amanda had experienced the night before. It had started over something that seemed so insignificant—a comment he had made over dinner about their plans to spend Christmas with his family. Amanda had fallen silent, and he had learned that this meant she was upset about something. "What's wrong?" he asked.

"Nothing," she replied.

"Then why do you have that look on your face? That's how you act when you're angry with me about something."

"I don't want to talk about it now," Amanda said.

"You never want to talk about it. Do you think that whatever is bothering you will just go away? Amanda, if there's a problem, we need to talk it out."

With that, Amanda went into the bedroom and locked the door. "So there I was . . ." Eric told Scott. "I pounded my fist on the door and said, 'We'll never get this resolved if you don't come out! You can't hide in there forever!' She just turned on the television and never left the room the rest of the night. I slept on the couch."

Scott cast a lure to a partially submerged log, hoping to coax a largemouth bass out of hiding. Then he turned to Eric. "Something tells me that you and Amanda go through this same pattern every time you have a problem," he said. "You want to get in there and work out the conflict, and she wants to run and hide."

"Right, she never wants to talk."

"Okay," Scott said, "let me ask you this: How is your communication at other times? Do you spend much time talking to each other?"

"About what?"

Scott smiled and said, "Maybe I just uncovered part of your problem."

1. Why do you think many couples experience little conflict during courtship and engagement?

_____

_____

_____

_____

_____

2. If you were Scott, what would you do to help Eric learn how to communicate with Amanda?

_____

_____

_____

_____

_____

 # GET THE TRUTH

Any engaged couple will argue or disagree about things. But often they are so caught up in the whirlwind of romance and wedding plans that they really don't experience much conflict. So they're surprised when the storm inevitably sweeps into their home.

While conflict is inevitable, one of the greatest values of courtship and engagement is the opportunity to develop your ability to communicate effectively. To avoid the "Post-Wedding Letdown," we suggest learning a few basic communication skills.

Listening to Understand

The Bible has much to say about the act of communicating, because God knew it would not be a skill that comes easily for us. We've got to work at it. But in doing so, we grow in our dependence upon Him and in our relationship with others.

1. State in your own words the listening principle found in each of the following passages of Scripture. Try to state the principles as complete sentences.

"But everyone must be quick to hear, slow to speak and slow to anger" (Jas. 1:19b).

Listening principle:

_____

_____

_____

_____

"A wise man will hear and increase in learning, a man of understanding will acquire wise counsel" (Prov. 1:5).

Listening principle:

_____

_____

_____

_____

2. What are some practical ways that you could apply these listening principles in your relationship right now?

_____

_____

_____

_____

_____

Listening is hard work. It requires hearing with more than our ears—we use our eyes and our hearts as well. That is why authentic communication requires proper listening habits.

Proper Listening Habits

Focus on . . .	Rather than . . .
What is being said	How you feel about what is said
The way it is being said: tone of voice, posture, and so on	The words only
Clarification of valid points	Defense of incorrect accusations
Questions	Indictments
Understanding	Judgment

Listening Questions

Clarifying questions: "Are you telling me that _____

_____?"

"What did you mean when you said

_____?"

Summary questions: "Of all that you just said, what do you most want me to understand?"
"What do you need from me most right now?"

3. How do you think that adopting proper listening habits and using appropriate listening questions would help you in resolving a conflict?

_____

_____

_____

_____

Expressing to Be Understood

4. State in your own words the principle found in each of the following Scriptures. Try to state the principles as complete sentences.

"Let no unwholesome word proceed from your mouth, but only such a word as is good for edification according to the need of the moment, that it may give grace to those who hear" (Eph. 4:29).

Speaking principle:

_____

_____

_____

_____

"When there are many words, transgression is unavoid-able, but he who restrains his lips is wise" (Prov. 10:19).

Speaking principle:

_____

_____

_____

"There is an appointed time for everything. And there is a time for every event under heaven . . . a time to be silent, and time to speak" (Eccles. 3:1,7b).

Speaking principle:

_____

_____

_____

5. What are some practical ways that you could apply these principles in your relationship right now?

_____

_____

_____

_____

_____

In the same way that we must actually seek clarification as a listener, we must also be deliberate with regard to what, how and when we choose to express ourselves. As a rule of thumb, consider the following steps toward expressing yourself:

Determine what you want to say.
   ♥ What are my assumptions?
   ♥ What are my beliefs?
   ♥ What are my desires?
   ♥ What are my dreams?
   ♥ What are my needs?

Determine how you want to say it.
   ♥ With excitement?
   ♥ With sadness?
   ♥ With conviction?
   ♥ With disappointment?
   ♥ With encouragement?

Determine when you should say it so that your communication will be most effective:
   ♥ During or after a meal
   ♥ During recreation
   ♥ At bedtime
   ♥ In the presence of children
   ♥ While driving

6. How do you think these speaking skills would help you in resolving a conflict?

_____

_____

_____

_____

_____

The Scriptures have a lot to say about the power of the tongue—and of the listening ear. If you want to develop an intimate marriage relationship, you would be wise to speak less and listen more. The person who speaks less is more willing to set his own self-centeredness aside and build oneness in a marriage. He is better able to understand another viewpoint. And he is willing to seek the best for his mate.

Resolving Conflict
All of the communications skills discussed so far in this chapter will prove invaluable in helping you resolve a conflict in your relationship. But there are two more important principles for you to apply:

7. What does the following verse have to say about resolving conflict?

"Be angry, and yet do not sin; do not let the sun go down on your anger" (Eph. 4:26).

Resolving conflict means . . .

_____

_____

_____

8. What happens in a relationship when this principle is not applied?

_____

_____

_____

In marriage, it's common for both individuals to react to conflict in different ways. Here are the four most common reactions:

- ♥ **Fight to win:** This is the "I win, you lose" or "I'm right, you're wrong" position. You seek to dominate the other person; personal relationships take second place to the need to triumph.

- ♥ **Withdraw:** You seek to avoid discomfort at all costs, saying, "I'm uncomfortable, so I'll get out." You see no hope of resolving the conflict, or you lack the strength to confront it. So you cope by giving your mate the silent treatment.

- ♥ **Yield:** You assume it is far better to go along with the other person's demands than to risk a confrontation. Rather than start another argument, you say, "Whatever you want is fine." To you, a safe feeling is more important than a close relationship.

♥ **Lovingly resolve:** You commit to resolving the conflict by taking steps to carefully and sensitively discuss the issue. Resolving a conflict requires a special attitude—one of humility, of placing the relationship at a higher priority than the conflict itself. You value your relationship more than winning or losing, escaping or feeling comfortable.

With three of these styles, you actually create as many problems as you solve. Fighting to win, withdrawing or yielding may allow you to deal temporarily with the conflict at hand, but you haven't really dealt with the emotions the conflict sparked—the hurt, the resentment and the anger. Only when you seek to confront each other in a loving way will you resolve a conflict.

9. What does the following verse have to say about resolving conflict?

   Be kind to one another, tender-hearted, forgiving each other, just as God in Christ also has forgiven you (Eph. 4:32).

   Resolving conflict means . . .

   _____

   _____

   _____

10. What will happen in a relationship when this principle is not applied?

    _____

    _____

Resolving conflict also requires forgiveness—giving up the right to punish the one who has wronged you. This is the miracle of the Christian life—that we can heal our relationships with others in the same way Christ healed our relationship with Him—through forgiveness.

NAVIGATING BY
TRUE NORTH:
Truths to Chart Your Course

♥ Authentic communication is much more than just talking. It is understanding, being understood, identifying a tone of voice, detecting nonverbal cues, responding appropriately to offense, resolving conflicts, knowing what to say, when to say it and how to say it. It is experiencing the risks and rewards of knowing and being known.

♥ Authentic communication means that the listener employs *clarifying* and *summary* questions.

♥ Resolving conflict requires a determination to lovingly confront each other.

♥ Resolving conflict requires forgiveness.

Couple's Project

 GET REAL

1. Spend a few minutes going through "Get the Picture" and "Get the Truth," sharing and discussing your answers to the different questions. Be sure to ask your fiancé(e) to explain the answers.

2. When there is static on the phone line, little communication takes place. What you say and what you hear is fuzzy, unclear and often unintelligible. In your everyday communication with your fiancé(e), you will find static of another kind. It has nothing to do with electricity, but it will short-circuit your communication just the same. If you fail to anticipate it and make adjustments, you will experience difficulty communicating.

   Each individual has a basic pattern of expressiveness. One is neither right nor wrong; each is simply different. And you must account for the differences between you and your fiancé(e) to communicate effectively.

   a. Individually, place an X where you think you fall on the continuum. Put an O where you think your fiancé(e) falls.

Pattern of Expression:

Fact Oriented   **Feeling Oriented**

1----2-----3-----4-----5-----6----7----8-----9----10
Rational and logical   Emotional and random

1----2-----3-----4-----5-----6----7----8-----9----10
Thinks "bottom line"   Thinks "this is how I feel"

1----2-----3-----4-----5-----6----7----8-----9----10
Difficulty expressing emotions   Passionate and expressive

    b. Discuss your answer with your fiancé(e). Do you agree or disagree?

    _____

    _____

    c. Describe a past discussion in which your differences or similarities in pattern of expression were obvious.

    _____

    _____

    _____

    Who said what?

    _____

    _____

    _____

    _____

    How was it said?

    _____

    _____

    _____

    _____

What happened as a result of the discussion?

_____

_____

_____

3. How was conflict resolved in your family as you grew up?

    _____

    _____

    _____

    _____

4. Which of the four conflict resolution styles do you adopt in most conflicts?

    ❑ Fight to win   ❑ Yield
    ❑ Withdraw   ❑ Lovingly resolve

5. Which of the four styles does your fiancé(e) usually adopt in conflicts?

    ❑ Fight to win   ❑ Yield
    ❑ Withdraw   ❑ Lovingly resolve

6. Have you seen unresolved conflict damage your relationship? How?

    _____

    _____

    _____

    _____

7. Do you feel you have trouble admitting when you are at fault? Does your fiancé(e)?

    _____

    _____

    _____

    _____

8. Do you have trouble expressing forgiveness? Does your fiancé(e)?

_____

_____

_____

Optional Communication Exercise: Share Your LifeMap

Take turns explaining your LifeMaps from the Understanding Your Personal History worksheet.

Keep in mind the principles you've already learned about authentic communication as you review your fiancé(e)'s Life-Map. Remember, don't just hear the words, but discern the tone of voice and nonverbal cues. Make sure you use clarifying and summary questions when appropriate. Finally, be sure your focus as a listener is on the right things.

Here are a few questions to ask about the major milestones your fiancé(e) describes in the LifeMap:

- How did that make you feel then?
- How does that make you feel now?
- What do you think God wants you to do with that?
- How do you think that event shaped your view of yourself physically, intellectually, socially, spiritually?
- Do you think you are still carrying emotions from that event today?
- In what ways did these things shape your dreams and desires?
- In what ways did these things shape your fears and anxieties?
- What have you learned from these experiences?
- In what ways are you who you are today because of these events?
- How do you see our relationship fitting into the ebb and flow of your LifeMap?

GET TO THE HEART
of Your Marriage

No doubt, by this point you are well aware of the spiritual nature of marriage. In this area of communication, it should come as no surprise that your communication with God will have a direct influence on your communication with your fiancé(e).

In this time of prayer, practice your listening skills by praying back to God what you hear Him saying in His Word to you.

1. As you kneel together, read the following verses silently to yourselves:

   How blessed is the man who does not walk in the counsel of the wicked, nor stand in the path of sinners, nor sit in the seat of scoffers!
   But his delight is in the law of the LORD, and in His law he meditates day and night.
   He will be like a tree firmly planted by streams of water, which yields its fruit in its season and its leaf does not wither; and in whatever he does, he prospers (Ps. 1:1-3).

2. After a few moments of silently reading and thinking about the passage, one of you should read the verses aloud.

3. Now say a prayer to God that reflects back to Him what He has expressed in the psalm.

   Example:

   Dear God,
   You say in Psalm 1 that a blessed person is someone who is serious about knowing and obeying Your Word. I want to be a person like that. Rather than listening to what others say, help me to listen to what You say. In Christ's name, Amen.

GET DEEPER

1. Read pages 201-209 in *Staying Close,* by Dennis and Barbara Rainey.

2. Complete the Couple Interview project on pages 241-243.

 # SPECIAL QUESTIONS
for Those Who Were Previously Married

1. In what ways do you think poor communication contributed to the failure of your first marriage? Bottom line, what mistakes did you make in the area of communication? (Look back at the principles learned in this chapter.)

   _____

   _____

   _____

   _____

2. List some reasons why you believe you will not make the same communication mistakes in this marriage.

   _____

   _____

   _____

   _____

3. What specific changes do you think you need to make in your communication style as you consider remarriage? What skills do you need to develop and practice? (Look back at the principles learned in this chapter.)

   _____

   _____

   _____

   _____

*For two people in a marriage to live together day after day is unquestionably
the one miracle the Vatican has overlooked.*

BILL COSBY

Chapter 6

Roles and Responsibilities

 TRUE NORTH

The Bible sets forth specific and distinct responsibilities for a husband and wife, which must be accurately understood and accurately fulfilled.

You're driving down a street, and from behind you comes the driving, thudding sound of music. A teenage driver has decided to give everyone within 500 yards the pleasure of listening to his music. You wonder how this kid could drive, or even think, with his sound system turned up so loud.

Discussing responsibilities for husbands and wives in marriage is like that. If you try to calmly explain a workable model to someone, the noise of our culture may easily drown you out. The irony is that every marriage settles into some type of social and organizational arrangement, with both husband and wife playing specific roles to uphold it. The question is whether these responsibilities should be defined by the God who created marriage or by the opinions of humans.

As you complete this chapter,[1] you will be given the opportunity to think and plan intentionally and biblically about your God-given roles as a husband or wife. In doing so, you'll begin to see the benefits of building your marriage on God's unchanging design.

GET THE PICTURE

1. What have been the "traditional" responsibilities for a husband and wife, as many people have understood them over the last few hundred years?

_____

_____

_____

2. Now think for a moment about how the media (especially television and films) generally portrays husbands and wives.

    a. Which of the following characters best describe, in your view, how wives are portrayed today? Think of an example, if possible. (Feel free to check more than one character.)

    _____ The Heroine   _____ The Martyr
    _____ The Victim   _____ The Extra
    _____ The Villain   _____ The Leader
    _____ The Brains   _____ The Tyrant
    _____ Other: _____

    Example:

    _____

    _____

    b. Which of the following characters best describe, in your view, how husbands are portrayed today? Think of an example, if possible. (Feel free to check more than one character.)

    _____ The Hero   _____ The Martyr
    _____ The Incompetent Idiot   _____ The Extra
    _____ The Villain   _____ The Leader
    _____ The Brawn (no brain)   _____ The Tyrant
    _____ The Pioneering Explorer
    _____ Other: _____

Example:

_____

_____

_____

3. Rank how each of the following influenced your understanding of roles or responsibilities in marriage. Use number 1 to represent the most influential voice. Use number
   6 to represent the least influential voice.

   _____ How I saw my parents live out their marriage
   _____ What I have observed from today's culture
   _____ How my peers have chosen to live out their
          marriages
   _____ What I've learned from the Bible and church
   _____ Things I have read, studied, seen
   _____ Other: _____

In our culture today, we see a backlash against traditional
roles. The idea that the husband should be the "leader" in a
marriage is seen as unjust, confining, cruel and antiquated.
Women have been encouraged to be more assertive and independent in marriage, and to seek fulfillment in their careers. In
many circles, a mother who stays at home with her children is
often portrayed as unintelligent and boring—wasting her time
"doing housework."

But few people are happy with the way responsibilities in
many marriages are handled today. As women become more
assertive in the marriage relationship, many men have become increasingly passive in their homes. Women then become less respectful of their husbands, and husbands in turn
show less love to their wives. Meanwhile, as our society grows
more sexually ambiguous, boys and girls grow up with little
concept of what it means to be a man or woman.

It's time to understand what the Bible says.

 GET THE TRUTH

Let's do a quick review. State God's purposes for marriage (refer to chapter 1, "Why Marriage?" if you need to):

Purpose number 1: _____

Purpose number 2: _____

Purpose number 3: _____

As we consider what the Bible has to say about responsibilities in marriage, it is important to remember that these are not arbitrary or cultural. These are not positions that denote privilege or rank, but rather *functions* in the context of teamwork—functions that are inseparably tied to God's purposes for marriage.

A Husband's Responsibilities

1. What do the following passages tell us about the responsibilities a husband should take on in the marriage relationship?

   For the husband is the head of the wife, as Christ also is the head of the church, He Himself being the Savior of the body (Eph. 5:23).

   Now I praise you because you remember me in everything, and hold firmly to the traditions, just as I delivered them to you. But I want you to understand that Christ is the head of every man, and the man is the head of a woman, and God is the head of Christ (1 Cor. 11:2-3).

   _____

   _____

   _____

   _____

2. What do you think it means that the husband is the head—the leader—of the wife "as Christ also is the head of the church"? What type of leadership did Christ display?

_____

_____

_____

A husband's leadership in marriage is not based on superior abilities but on divine placement. Leadership means assuming responsibility for the relationship, being accountable to God and putting your wife's needs above your own. It means making her load lighter, not heavier. It means helping her develop and utilize her gifts and abilities. It means loving her sacrificially.

3. It's important to understand that true biblical leadership is much different from what the world believes. What key words or phrases describe the two types of leaders in this passage?

Calling them to Himself, Jesus said to them, "You know that those who are recognized as rulers of the Gentiles lord it over them; and their great men exercise authority over them. But it is not this way among you, but whoever wishes to become great among you shall be your servant; and whoever wishes to be first among you shall be slave of all. For even the Son of Man did not come to be served, but to serve, and to give His life a ransom for many" (Mark 10:42-45).

Jesus' Leadership	Gentile Leadership

4. What additional insight can you gain from the following verse about what it means for a man to lead his wife?

Husbands, love your wives, just as Christ also loved the church and gave Himself up for her (Eph. 5:25).

_____
_____
_____
_____
_____

In the marriage relationship, Gods call the husband to be a servant-leader who takes the initiative to direct his family and serve the needs of his wife and children. A servant-leader, for example, takes the initiative to be the spiritual leader in the home—to pray, to worship at church and to study God's Word. He takes the initiative to provide for his family and make sure finances are in order. He takes the initiative to ask forgiveness, resolve conflict and ensure that his home is a place of encouragement and safety.

5. Complete the following chart that contrasts the way a servant-leader, a lording-leader and a passive non-leader would handle everyday situations at home.

SITUATION	LORDING LEADER	PASSIVE NON-LEADER	SERVANT-LEADER
The couple needs to purchase a new automobile.	He buys what he wants without considering what his wife and family need.	He puts off the discussion and the decision. He leaves all the shopping and research up to his wife, then becomes non-communicative or angry when he doesn't like the choice.	He deliberates with his wife, making a joint decision based on both of their input and desires. He puts the needs of the family before his own personal preference.

The husband arrives home and the house is messy and dinner is not prepared.			
Facing a huge bill for car repairs, the couple grows discouraged about whether God will provide for their needs.			
The husband wants to go camping in the mountains for vacation, but the wife prefers going to a beach resort.			

A Wife's Responsibilities

6. What do the following passages tell us about the responsibilities of a woman in marriage?

Wives, be subject to your own husbands, as to the Lord. For the husband is the head of the wife, as Christ also is the head of the church, He Himself being the Savior of the body. But as the church is subject to Christ, so also the wives ought to be subject to their husbands in everything (Eph. 5:22-24).

Then the LORD God said, "It is not good for the man to be alone: I will make him a helper suitable for him" (Gen. 2:18).

Older women likewise are to be reverent in their behavior, not malicious gossips, nor enslaved to much wine, teaching what is good, that they may encourage the young women to love their husbands, to love their children, to be sensible, pure, workers at home, kind, being subject to their own husbands, so that the word of God may not be dishonored (Titus 2:3-5).

The wife must see to it that she respects her husband (Eph. 5:33b).

These passages speak of a wife's responsibility to demonstrate love for her husband by respecting and supporting him. Respect is a choice to receive your husband in spite of his weaknesses. Supporting your husband—being subject or submissive to his leadership—is a choice to complement him rather than compete with him. It does not mean you are inferior, that you lose your identity or that you ignore your own gifts. And it does not mean you blindly obey or submit to verbal or physical abuse; and it does not mean following a husband into sin. Instead, it means giving up your desire to control and cooperating with him as he seeks to lead your marriage and family.

John Piper writes, "Submission is the divine calling of a wife to honor and affirm her husband's leadership and help carry it through according to her gifts. . . . It is an attitude that says, 'I delight for you to take the initiative in our family. I am glad when you take responsibility for things and lead with love. I don't flourish in the relationship when you are passive and I have to make sure the family works.'"[2]

7. For Women Only: Does an accurate definition of the man's responsibilities as servant-leader make the thought of submission easier and more reasonable? Why or why not?

_____
_____
_____

8. Let's look again at Genesis 2:18, which tells us, "Then the Lord God said, 'It is not good for the man to be alone; I will make him a helper suitable for him.'"

   What type of value does our culture place on the role of "helper"? Why?

   _____
   _____
   _____

9. Circle the term "helper" in each of the following passages:

   Behold, God is my helper; The Lord is the sustainer of my soul (Ps. 54:4).

   But the Helper, the Holy Spirit, whom the Father will send in My name, He will teach you all things, and bring to your remembrance all that I said to you (John 14:26).

   The Lord is my helper, I will not be afraid. What will man do to me? (Heb. 13:6).

10. How does knowing that God describes Himself as a helper change the way a wife could feel about being called a helper?

    _____
    _____
    _____

An accurate understanding of the role of a wife as helper shows how vital the role is in providing what is lacking in a man. Husbands have gaps in their lives that their wives are uniquely qualified to fill.

11. What are some ways a husband needs his wife's help?

_____

_____

_____

The opposite of being a helper is being a competitor. Competitors do the opposite of filling gaps and supporting weak areas. They exploit those weaknesses to gain the upper hand. A competitive wife can stir a husband to aggression and retaliation or to withdrawal rather than caring, supporting and meeting the woman's need.

At stake here is an organizational structure that God created to make a marriage work. God designed a woman as a completer for her husband. Man is to be a self-denying servant-leader of his wife. And when a husband and wife are fulfilling these roles in marriage, they honor God. They glorify Him, which is one of the purposes of the institution of marriage.

12. What do the following verses tell us about how a husband should respond to his wife as she fulfills her responsibilities?

Her husband . . . praises her, saying: "Many daughters have done nobly, but you excel them all" (Prov. 31:28-29).

Show her honor as a fellow heir of the grace of life (1 Pet. 3:7).

_____

_____

_____

_____

13. Why is a husband's response of praise and honor so crucial to the success of a wife pursuing her biblical role? What will happen if she doesn't receive this from her husband?

_____

_____

_____

_____

NAVIGATING BY
TRUE NORTH:
Truths to Chart Your Course

♥ Every marriage settles into some type of social and organizational arrangement, with both husband and wife playing specific roles to uphold it. Bottom line: *There are no roleless marriages.*

♥ The Bible sets forth specific and distinct responsibilities for a husband and wife in marriage.

♥ A husband is called to be a servant-leader in marriage, leading as Christ leads and loving as Christ loves.

♥ A wife is called to respect and support her husband, completing his leadership and filling the gaps in his life.

Notes
1. This chapter is adapted from the HomeBuilders Couples Series, Robert Lewis and David Boehi, *Building Teamwork in Your Marriage* (Little Rock, AR: FamilyLife Publishing, 2010).
2. John Piper, "The Beautiful Faith of Fearless Submission," sermon delivered April 15, 2007, http://www.desiringgod.org/ResourceLibrary/Sermons/ByDate/2007/2088_The_Beautiful_Faith_of_Fearless_Submission/.

Couple's Project

 GET REAL

Interact as a couple around the following activities.

1. Spend a few minutes going through "Get the Picture" and "Get the Truth," sharing and discussing your answers to the different questions. Be sure to ask your fiancé(e) to explain the answers.

2. (Note: This question is also found in the "Understanding Your Personal History" worksheet.) What roles did your parents assume in the home when you were growing up?

    a. Who was the leader in the marriage?

    _____
    _____
    _____

    b. Who was the leader as a parent?

    _____
    _____
    _____

    c. How did they make decisions?

    _____
    _____

3. At this time, how well do you believe you and your fiancé(e) are in agreement with God's design for a husband's and wife's distinct and specific responsibilities?

Not Aligned   **Very Aligned**

1 - - - 2 - - - - 3 - - - - 4 - - - - - 5 - - - - 6 - - - - - 7 - - - - 8 - - - - 9 - - - - 10

Explain:

_____

_____

_____

_____

_____

_____

4. Experiencing the positive power of core responsibilities fulfilled:

a. Men: Tell your fiancée about a time when you experienced her as a helper who filled gaps in your life. How did it make you feel?

_____

_____

_____

_____

b. Women: Tell your fiancé about a time when you experienced him as a servant-leader who took the initiative for your good. How did it make you feel?

_____

_____

_____

_____

5. Experiencing the *negative* power of core roles unfulfilled:

   a. Men: Tell your fiancé(e) about a time when you experienced her as a competitor rather than a helper. How did it make you feel?

   b. Women: Tell your fiancé(e) about a time when you needed him to take the initiative but he did not, or a time when you felt he was a lording leader or passive non-leader rather than a servant-leader. How did it make you feel?

6. Conflict over responsibilities in marriage often centers on two areas: making important decisions and dividing work around the house. What insights have you gained in this chapter that could help you avoid conflict in these areas?

GET TO THE HEART
of Your Marriage: Prayer

Only by the power of God will you be able to fulfill your responsibilities in marriage.

1. Take a few moments, and using the sample prayer as a springboard, pray together, expressing your desire to fulfill the unique role God has given each of you in marriage. Rather than praying for your fiancé(e) to fulfill his or her role, pray for yourself, that you would take responsibility in your role and your response.

2. Sample Prayer

   Here is a sample of what the man might pray:

   Dear God,
   The high and privileged role You have called me to as a servant-leader is something I want to strive for. There are many areas I need to develop in, many areas I need to take more responsibility for. Help me to love my fiancée as Christ loved the church and to serve her sacrificially. Bring to mind ways that I can praise and esteem her as my future helpmate. In Christ's name, amen.

 # GET DEEPER

Here are two special optional assignments for those who want to go deeper.

1. Complete the Roles Position Statement (page 181).

2. For a more in-depth look at roles, read *Rocking the Roles*, by Robert Lewis, and *Love and Respect*, by Emerson Eggerichs. (These resources are available through FamilyLife at 1-800-FL-TODAY or www.familylife.com.)

SPECIAL QUESTIONS
for Those Who Were Previously Married

Answer these questions individually (if applicable), then share your answers with your fiancé(e).

1. How were husband/wife responsibilities handled in your previous marriage?

   _____

   _____

   _____

   _____

2. Can you think of some ways that your view and practice of gender responsibilities in your previous marriage are affecting your current relationship?

   _____

   _____

   _____

   _____

3. List at least three specific things you will do in this marriage to fulfill your biblical responsibilities that you may have failed to do in your previous marriage.

   _____

   _____

   _____

   _____

Optional

Roles Position Statement

There is nothing nobler or more admirable than when two people who see eye to eye keep house as man and wife, confounding their enemies and delighting their friends.

HOMER

The issue of roles in marriage is a volatile subject. Knowing *what* you believe about role responsibilities in marriage and *why* you believe it is one of the strongest statements you will make as a couple to the world around you.

This project will provide you the opportunity to formulate and formalize what you believe about this critical subject. Developing a clear, concise statement of belief will prove to be a refuge and an encouragement as you seek to build your marriage according to God's design.

Chances are this will not be the only time you will grapple with these issues. You may want to work through this project again after you are married and have some experience working out your responsibilities.

Instructions

1. Individually, prepare a Position Statement on two topics:

   ♥ What you believe about responsibilities for a husband and wife in marriage. Include biblical references that support *why* you believe as you do.

♥ How you will live those beliefs out in your marriage.
  Make this very practical.

2. Refer back to your notes in this chapter to formulate your
   position. Be sure to cite your biblical reasons for why you
   hold a certain position.

3. Try to make each section a short and concise paragraph.
   Both statements, typed out, should not exceed a half sheet
   of paper.

4. After you have completed your own personal statement,
   meet with your fiancé(e) to compare your statements. Together, hammer out a final statement that the two of you
   can agree represents what you, together, believe about
   roles in marriage. This Position Statement will read,
   "What we believe . . ."

Responsibilities of a Husband and Wife in Marriage

What we believe:

_____
_____
_____
_____
_____
_____
_____
_____

How our beliefs will be lived out in our marriage:

_____
_____
_____
_____
_____
_____
_____
_____

_____ Date _____

_____ Date _____

Witnessed/affirmed

_____ Date _____

There are three conversions:
the conversion of the heart, the mind, and the purse.

MARTIN LUTHER

Chapter 7

Money, Money, Money

 TRUE NORTH
God owns it all. We are stewards of His resources.

If you want to test a couple's oneness in marriage, take a look
at how they handle their finances. It may be the most important test any couple faces in marriage.

For years, surveys have shown that couples list finances as
one of the leading causes of divorce. And it's usually not the
lack of money that causes problems; it's how they handle it
and how they communicate about it.

How a person handles his money reveals much about his
character, his desires, his priorities and his relationship with
God. Put two people together in marriage, and you can see that
financial discussions are really spiritual discussions.

Married couples work most of their lives at communicating
with one another about financial issues. Decisions on spending,
saving, tithing, investing, hobbies, allowances and many other
related issues are all hammered out over the years together.

But many of you probably find managing your finances a
challenge even as a single person. You can save yourselves a
great deal of conflict after the wedding day if you discuss a few
key issues now.

In this chapter, you will uncover the secrets of true con-
tentment when it comes to money and material possessions.
You will have the opportunity as a couple to think through
your attitudes, hopes and plans in this critical area of finances.

This chapter won't solve the future challenges you'll face around money, but it will give you some foundational truths and basic skills you need to apply to your lives.

GET THE PICTURE

Read the following case study and respond to the questions that follow.

Case Study: Eric and Amanda's Financial Adventure

Eric and Amanda's financial challenges began as newlyweds. Each day as they drove home from work to their small apartment, they saw a slick billboard. It pictured a beautiful home with a bold statement: "YOUR FAMILY DESERVES THE BEST."

With many of their friends buying homes in the new Mercer Lake development, it seemed like a great time to buy a home. Their friends reinforced this idea with comments like, "Boy, it's great to be out of our old apartment!" and "How do you manage to live in such a cramped space?" Amanda kept saying to Eric, "It sure would be nice to have a place of our own."

One day they heard that their wedding photos were ready. That night after work, Eric and Amanda eagerly rushed down to the studio to pick up the album. The pictures looked great and brought back many wonderful memories of their wedding day. However, the sting came when Eric looked at the photographer's bill. He began to feel the pressure of other bills they were facing from their honeymoon in Cancun: hotels, airfare, restaurants, gifts. But Eric didn't say anything about it to Amanda; he didn't want to spoil a great moment.

Amanda, meanwhile, was feeling a different pressure. Thanksgiving was approaching, and Eric's family would be joining them for the day. It really would be nice, she thought, if they could complete their set of china. "Eric, we could finish the set with just $300. In fact, that would allow us to entertain more often." Eric thought again of the other bills he hadn't mentioned to Amanda, but agreed to let her spend the money.

In the months ahead, Eric started to feel their finances were getting away from them. Their credit card bills were running up from their furniture and clothing purchases.

"Amanda, we have got to try a budget!" Eric said. But after a couple of months they gave up keeping track of their expenses, and they finally set the budget notebook aside. "It's too tedious," Eric moaned.

In late spring, they received an offer of a $200 gift certificate to a department store, plus dinner for two at a nice restaurant. All they needed to do was to take a two-hour tour with a real-estate agent at the Mercer Lake development. They agreed to take the tour so they could receive the free gifts.

During the tour they were extremely impressed with the homes. They found one they especially liked, and the agent mentioned that it was on sale at a "special low price"—but only for that day.

They talked for a few minutes and decided to purchase the home. "We'll find a way to get by," they reasoned. "And if we have to sell at a later date, we'll make a profit. We've got to take some risks to get ahead."

In the next five months they began to quarrel more and more about money. Amanda believed that Eric was spending too much money on frivolous purchases for himself. In anger he turned the finances over to Amanda: "If you are so smart, you take care of the bills!"

Then a golden opportunity came. Eric was offered a promotion at work. The salary was much higher, but it meant he would be away from home three nights a week and one weekend each month.

The payments on the house mortgage were stretching them, but with both salaries they could make it, and even eat out a couple times each week. Then one day, Amanda asked Eric a question that would change their lives forever: "Eric, do you think we should paint the extra bedroom pink or blue?"

They celebrated the news of her pregnancy at their favorite restaurant. On the drive home, Eric pondered the thought of a little boy to play golf with someday. Amanda smiled to herself, imagining a little girl playing dolls and serving make-believe tea.

But in the quietness of the car and the cool evening breeze, a nagging question disturbed their thoughts: *How will we make it if Amanda has to stop working?*

1. What are some of the mistakes you think Eric and Amanda made in their finances?

   _____
   _____
   _____
   _____
   _____
   _____

2. What attitudes or pressures led them to make these decisions?

   _____
   _____
   _____
   _____
   _____
   _____

3. Make your own list of the financial mistakes you think you could most likely make in your first years of marriage. These can be attitudes, actions or beliefs.

My Top Five Concerns

a. _____
b. _____
c. _____
d. _____
e. _____

The mistakes Eric and Amanda made were all too common for married couples. Many people become adults with little training in how to handle money. They don't know how to set priorities; they are influenced by the culture and by their peers, and they lack the basic discipline they need to set and keep a budget. Most important, they lack God's perspective on finances.

 GET THE TRUTH

When discussing finances, there are two foundational questions you must answer to gain a biblical perspective on money. Without them, you are left to the winds of culture and the impulsive and unpredictable passions of your heart to guide you.

Who Does This Money Belong to?

1. Read the following passages and circle the phrases in these passages that indicate ownership.

The earth is the LORD's and all it contains, the world, and those who dwell in it (Ps. 24:1).

Yours, O LORD, is the greatness and the power and the glory and the victory and the majesty, indeed everything that is in the heavens and the earth; Yours is the dominion, O LORD, and You exalt Yourself as head over all. Both riches and honor come from You. . . . For all things come from You, and from Your hand we have given You. . . . O LORD our God, all this abundance that we have provided to build You a house for Your holy name, it is from Your hand, and all is Yours (1 Chron. 29:11-12,14,16).

2. How should the truth that God owns everything affect the way you view material possessions and financial resources? Give a specific example of how you should apply this in your marriage.

_____
_____
_____
_____
_____
_____
_____

3. Critique the following statement:

"I'll give God 10 percent of my income and spend the other 90 percent as I please."

_____
_____
_____
_____
_____

It is natural and human to feel that what we earn is ours. But the Scriptures make it clear that the first foundational truth we must embrace is that God owns it all.

If God Is the Owner, What Does That Make Me?

4. What does the following passage say about our responsibility for the resources God has given us?

He who is faithful in a very little thing is faithful also in much; and he who is unrighteous in a very little thing is unrighteous also in much. Therefore if you have not been faithful in the use of unrighteous wealth, who will entrust the true riches to you? And if you have not been faithful in the use of that which is another's, who will give you that which is your own? No servant can serve two masters; for either he will hate the one and love the other, or else he will hold to one and despise the other. You cannot serve God and wealth (Luke 16:10-13).

5. The second foundational truth regarding finances flows from the first. If God owns it all, then we are not owners—we are stewards of His resources. What are the marks of a steward according to the passage we just read from Luke?

_____
_____
_____
_____

A steward is a person who manages another's property, finances or other affairs. A steward acts as a supervisor or administrator, of finances or property, for another. As financial advisor Ron Blue wrote, "Stewardship is the management of God's resources for the accomplishment of God-given goals."[1]

6. Another foundational truth regarding finances is found in the same Luke 16:10-13 passage we just read: You cannot serve both God and riches. What additional insight does the following passage add?

Do not store up for yourselves treasures on earth, where moth and rust destroy, and where thieves break in and steal. But store up for yourselves treasures in heaven, where neither moth nor rust destroys, and where thieves do not break in or steal; for where your treasure is, there your heart will be also (Matt. 6:19-21).

_____

_____

_____

_____

7. Give an example of someone who tried to store up treasures on earth rather than heaven. What ultimately happened to that person?

_____

_____

_____

_____

8. There is one more scriptural truth about finances that couples need to remember as they build their marriage: God not only owns it all, but He is also the one who supplies our needs.

_____

_____

_____

_____

Read the following passage:

For this reason I say to you, do not be worried about your life, as to what you will eat or what you will drink; nor for your body, as to what you will put on. Is not life more than food, and the body more than clothing? Look at the birds of the air, that they do not sow, nor reap nor gather into barns, and yet your heavenly Father feeds them. Are you not worth much more than they? And who of you by being worried can add a single hour to his life? And why are you worried about clothing? Observe how the lilies of the field grow; they do not toil nor do they spin, yet I say to you that not even Solomon in all his glory clothed himself like one of these. But if God so clothes the grass of the field, which is alive today and tomorrow is thrown into the furnace, will He not much more clothe you? You of little faith! Do not worry then, saying, "What will we eat?" or "What will we drink?" or "What will we wear for clothing?" For the Gentiles eagerly seek all these things; for your heavenly Father knows that you need all these things. But seek first His kingdom and His righteousness, and all these things will be added to you (Matt. 6:25-33).

a. Do you find it easy or difficult to turn your anxieties about money over to God?

_____

_____

_____

_____

b. Do you find it easy or difficult to live within your means—to live according to what God has provided—without going into debt?

_____

_____

_____

_____

Spiritual Decisions

Because we are stewards of the resources God has entrusted to us, every financial decision you make is actually a spiritual decision. For many, that's a revolutionary concept. How you manage your finances is a pretty good barometer for the condition of your spiritual life.

9. Based on what you've learned in this chapter, how do you think you might apply those principles to each of the following areas?

    a. Forming, maintaining and living within a budget:

_____
_____
_____

    b. Cost of the wedding and honeymoon:

_____
_____
_____

    c. Type of lifestyle you will lead as a couple after marriage:

_____
_____
_____
_____

    d. Giving to God's work:

_____
_____
_____
_____

    e. Debt:

_____
_____
_____
_____

The fact is that knowing God's perspective on finances should influence every area of your money management. You will realize, for example, that you have a responsibility to live within the means God has given you. You will look closely at your attitudes about material possessions and be more strict about your purchases. And you will free up more resources to go toward making God's work possible.

In the context of these truths—that *God owns it all* and *we are stewards of His resources*—you will hammer out money issues over a lifetime. And in developing a biblical view of finances together as a team, you will experience one of the great privileges and joys of marriage.

As we said earlier, how you handle money in your marriage may be the biggest test of your relationship. Now, before your wedding, is the time to commit to oneness in your finances.

This means:

- ♥ Viewing money as "ours" rather than "mine"
- ♥ Being open and honest about finances and not keeping secrets about income, spending, assets, debt, and so on
- ♥ Forming a budget together and working together to keep to it
- ♥ Making important financial decisions together
- ♥ Setting financial goals together

Finances can spark a fire in marriage that grows in intensity until the marriage is engulfed in a seemingly irreversible firestorm. Or it creates a spark of a different sort. In a oneness marriage, this spark of understanding, when fanned by the commitment to do God's will together, can blaze into the realization that you have the incredible privilege and responsibility of working together to manage His money for His eternal purposes.

NAVIGATING BY
TRUE NORTH:
Truths to Chart Your Course

♥ God owns it all and we are stewards of His resources.

♥ God supplies all of our needs.

♥ Every financial decision we make is actually a spiritual decision.

♥ Money is not an end in itself. It is a tool to be used to accomplish God's plans and purposes.

♥ Our attitude about money will drive our actions regarding money.

♥ The root issue in finances is never the amount of money; it is the attitude we have toward money.

♥ How we handle finances together may be the biggest test of oneness in our marriage.

Note
1. Ron Blue, *Splitting Heirs: Giving Your Money and Things to Your Children* (Chicago, IL: Northfield Publishing, 2004).

Couple's Project

 GET REAL

1. Spend a few minutes going through "Get the Picture" and "Get the Truth," sharing and discussing your answers to the different questions. Be sure to ask your fiancé(e) to explain the answers.

2. Rate yourself and your fiancé(e) on the following statement. Put an X where you would rate yourself and then place an O where you would rate your fiancé(e).

   a. My present attitude and practice reflect the biblical truths that God owns it all and I am a steward of the resources He entrusts to me.

   Poorly reflects   **Strongly reflects**

   1 - - - 2 - - - 3 - - - - 4 - - - 5 - - - 6 - - - - 7 - - - 8 - - - 9 - - - 10

   Explain:

   _____

   _____

   _____

   _____

   _____

b. My fiancé(e)'s attitude and practice reflect the biblical truths that God owns it all and he or she is a steward of the resources God entrusts to him or her.

Poorly reflects   **Strongly reflects**

1 - - - 2 - - - 3 - - - - 4 - - - - 5 - - - 6 - - - - 7 - - - - 8 - - - 9 - - - 10

Explain:

_____

_____

_____

_____

_____

_____

3. Work through the following chart by choosing the descriptions that best fit you and your fiancé(e). Then share your answers and discuss potential areas of conflict.

You		Fiancé(e)
	I'll buy it when I need it.	
	Buy it now while it's on sale and save.	
	K-Mart, blue light specials, generic is the way to go!	
	Malls, specialty boutiques—I only go for name brands.	
	Gas is gas; who cares where you buy it?	
	Gas is three cents cheaper down the street.	
	I'm within $50 of reconciling the checkbook this month—awesome!!	
	I'm not spending anything else until I discover that nickel discrepancy between my checkbook and the bank statement.	

	We shouldn't go to the movies tonight because we've spent our entertainment money for the month.	
	I'm a little over in this area of the budget, so I'm borrowing from next month.	

Most couples find that they differ significantly in a number of these areas. But remember that your differences are what can bond you together.

Your aim is not to change your fiancé(e) so that he or she approaches financial issues just like you. The aim is for both of you to work from the same biblical foundation: God owns it all, and we are stewards of His resources.

4. Write a brief statement about the most important insights you have gained about biblical principles of money from this chapter.

_____

_____

_____

_____

 GET TO THE HEART
of Your Marriage

5. Individually, make a list of seven material possessions that you value highly. Be specific (my television, my savings, my car, my grandmother's china, and so on). Then share your lists with each other.

_____

_____

_____

_____

_____

6. One way to acknowledge that, indeed, "God owns it all" is to express that fact in prayer. Take a moment right now and make a statement to God that you understand these possessions are in fact His possessions. Your prayer might sound something like this:

   Lord, I want You to know that I believe You own everything. And that includes everything on my list. And because it is all Yours, I want to thank You for entrusting these things to me.

Each of you can join the other as you express this prayer to God.

SPECIAL QUESTIONS
for Those Who Were Previously Married

Answer these questions individually, and then share your answers with your fiancé(e).

1. What lessons did you learn about financial issues in your first marriage that will be helpful as you prepare to marry again?

   _____

   _____

   _____

   _____

   _____

2. In what ways will continuing financial obligations related to your first marriage affect your new marriage, and how will you handle these?

   _____

   _____

   _____

   _____

   _____

3. If you receive any type of financial support from a previous spouse, how will that income be handled in your new marriage?

_____

_____

_____

_____

_____

_____

4. Are there any material possessions from your previous marriage (home, pictures, sentimental objects, and the like) that trouble your fiancé(e)? Discuss what to do with these.

_____

_____

_____

_____

_____

_____

Bonus

Setting a Budget

As you approach your wedding date, go ahead and set up a budget that will allow you to control your finances from the very beginning of your marriage.

As you fill in the blanks, here are some key questions to ask yourself:

- ♥ Are we saving enough for long-term needs?
- ♥ Can we stay out of debt with this budget?
- ♥ What do we have to sacrifice in order to stick with this budget?
- ♥ If the wife became pregnant, could you live on the income of the husband?

Household Budget

Date	Monthly Income $		
Budget Category	Monthly	Other than monthly	Total
Housing			
Mortgage/rent			
Insurance			
Property taxes			
Electricity			
Gas			
Water			
Sanitation			
Cleaning			
Telephone			
Repairs/maintenance			
Supplies			
Other			
Total			

Budget Category	Monthly	Other than monthly	Total
Food			
Clothing			
Transportation			
Insurance			
Gas and oil			
Maintenance/repairs			
Parking			
Other			
Total			

Budget Category	Monthly	Other than monthly	Total
Entertainment/Recreation			
Eating out			
Movies, concerts, etc.			
Baby-sitters			
Magazines/newspapers			
Vacations			
Clubs/activities			
Other			
Total			

Budget Category	Monthly	Other than monthly	Total
Medical Expenses			
Doctor			
Dentist			
Insurance			
Medication			
Other			
Total			

Budget Category	Monthly	Other than monthly	Total
Other Insurance			
Life			
Disability			
Other			
Total			

Budget Category	Monthly	Other than monthly	Total
Children			
Tuition			
School lunches			
Allowances			
Lessons/activities			
Other			
Total			

Budget Category	Monthly	Other than monthly	Total
Gifts			
Christmas			
Birthdays			
Anniversaries			
Other			
Total			

Budget Category	Monthly	Other than monthly	Total
Miscellaneous			
Toiletries			
Husband misc.			
Wife misc.			
Cleaning, laundry			
Animal care			
Hair care			
Other			
Total			
Total Living Expenses			

Contrary to [what some believe], sex is not a sin. Contrary to
Hugh Hefner, it's not salvation either. Like nitroglycerin,
it can be used either to blow up bridges or to heal hearts.

FREDERICK BUECHNER

We feasted on love; every mode of it, solemn and merry, romantic and realistic,
sometimes as dramatic as a thunderstorm, sometimes comfortable and unem-
phatic as putting on your soft slippers. She was my pupil and my teacher, my
subject and my sovereign, my trusty comrade, friend, shipmate, fellow-soldier.
My mistress, but at the same time all that any man friend has ever been to me.

C. S. LEWIS

Chapter 8

Intimacy:
Sexual Communication in Marriage

 TRUE NORTH
Sex is God's idea.

It's nearly impossible today to go for long without hearing or seeing some reference to sex. We live in a media-saturated culture, and our media is saturated with sex.

You see it in the plots of movies and television shows. In the suggestive commercials for erectile dysfunction. In the images in magazines and those flooding the Internet. In the links to pornographic websites offering fantasies at the click of a mouse. In the mainstream magazines with articles like, "Five Sex Secrets Women Wish Their Husbands Knew."

Sex has become a cultural obsession. But the picture of sexual intimacy that our culture paints is a cheap counterfeit and a perversion of God's original design. Like a surgeon's knife that has been designed for good but can be used for harm if put in the wrong hands, sex has been twisted and torn from its original purposes with devastating consequences.

In this chapter, you will catch a glimpse of the incredible privilege that God has given us in sexual intimacy. You'll uncover some possible misconceptions and replace them with God's perspective from the Scriptures. You will have the opportunity to talk about some of your fears and expectations.

And you will gain an appreciation for your unique, God-given design as a man or a woman and how your differences in this area will continue to strengthen your marriage bond.

 # GET THE PICTURE

Understanding the Past

1. What percentage of your sex education was received at each of the following "schools"? (Your total should equal 100 percent.)

    ___% Peer school: My friends talked about what we thought, knew or had heard.

    ___% Home school: My parents explained to me what sex is.

    ___% Private school: I read things on my own or asked certain people (not my parents).

    ___% Christian school: Church, Sunday School or youth group.

    ___% School of hard knocks: I learned by experience.

    ___% School of the silver screen: I learned from movies or television.

    ___% School of _____

    100% total

2. What are some of the *helpful* things that you learned in these schools?

    _____
    _____
    _____
    _____
    _____
    _____

3. What are some of the *harmful* things that you learned in these schools?

_____

_____

_____

_____

Special Note: Many people wonder how much of their sexual history they should disclose. If this is a concern for you, read the special section at the end of this chapter, "How Much Should I Share About My Past?" It will give you some guidelines on the appropriate level of disclosure regarding your sexual experience.

4. In our culture today, why do you think it is so important to learn what the Bible says about the sexual relationship?

_____

_____

_____

_____

The unfortunate fact is that most of us have received a poor sex education. Our knowledge, our viewpoints and our experiences are twisted by our culture; we learn about sex from man's perspective. In order to build a good sexual relationship when you are married, you need to learn what the Creator had in mind.

GET THE TRUTH

Once again, let's return to Genesis for some clues about God's view of sex:

> Therefore shall a man leave his father and his mother, and shall cleave unto his wife: and they shall be one flesh (Gen. 2:24, *ASV*).

Note the term "one flesh." You will recall from chapter 2 that this phrase is the origin of the word "oneness." Becoming one flesh involves deep relational intimacy of which sexual intercourse is an integral part.

Dr. Louis Evans, Jr., wrote about the term "one flesh":

> The one flesh in marriage is not just a physical phenomenon, but a uniting of the totality of two personalities. In marriage, we are one flesh spiritually by vow, economically by sharing, logistically by adjusting time and agreeing on the disbursement of all life's resources, experientially by trudging through the dark valleys and standing victoriously on the peaks of success, and sexually by the bonding of our bodies.[1]

Sex is not just a physical act. God created it as a process of intimate communication, of which the act of physical intercourse is a significant part. It is a powerful, emotional, bonding experience designed to strengthen a marriage much as metal rods reinforce concrete.

Premarital sex is so common in our culture today that some people are considered odd if they maintain their purity until marriage. But, as we discussed in the section on "A Special Word on Sexual Purity and Cohabitation" (see pages 97-104), God has our best in mind when He commands us to not engage in sex before marriage. He wants us to experience the absolute best, rather than a poor counterfeit.

The Right Purposes

For each of the following verses, state in your own words the purpose you see that God has for sex in marriage.

Purpose Number One

> God blessed them [Adam and Eve]; and God said to them, "Be fruitful and multiply, and fill the earth" (Gen. 1:28).

Behold, children are a gift of the LORD; the fruit of the womb is a reward. Like arrows in the hand of a warrior, so are the children of one's youth. How blessed is the man whose quiver is full of them (Ps. 127:3-5a).

1. According to these verses, one purpose God has for sex is:

_____

_____

_____

Purpose Number Two

Let your fountain be blessed, and rejoice in the wife of your youth. As a loving hind and a graceful doe, let her breasts satisfy you at all times; be exhilarated always with her love (Prov. 5:18-19).

2. According to this verse, a second purpose God has for sex is:

_____

_____

_____

Purpose Number Three

But because of immoralities, each man is to have his own wife, and each woman is to have her own husband. The husband must fulfill his duty to his wife, and likewise also the wife to her husband. The wife does not have authority over her own body, but the husband does; and likewise also the husband does not have authority over his own body, but the wife does. Stop depriving one another, except by agreement for a time, so that you may devote yourselves to prayer, and come together again so that Satan will not tempt you because of your lack of self-control (1 Cor. 7:2-5).

3. A third purpose God has for sex in marriage is:

_____

_____

_____

Your answers probably could be summed up by three key words:

Procreation: Sex is intended for the creation of children. God's command to "be fruitful and multiply" has not changed or been revoked.

Pleasure: Sex is intended for the pleasure and enjoyment of the man and woman. Contrary to the interpretations of the medieval church, God is the author of sexual pleasure, not the censor.

Protection: Sex is intended to protect a husband and wife from temptation. Failure to sexually satisfy each other in marriage can lead to a spouse looking outside the marriage for fulfillment.

4. Which of these purposes is a surprise or a new insight to you?

_____

_____

How does this new understanding affect your view of sex?

_____

_____

_____

5. Do you have any difficulty accepting any of these purposes for sex? If so, why?

_____

_____

_____

Understanding Your Differences

Researchers continue to observe consistent differences in the attitudes, needs and responses men and women bring into a sexual relationship. This confirms how God created us "male" and "female." We are different and distinct.

Understanding these differences in the sexual area is foundational to developing a healthy, mutually satisfying sex life.

6. Read through the following chart and circle anything that particularly interests you, or something you did not realize before.

Note: These are general, commonly observed differences between men and women, and not concrete facts. Don't use this chart to determine how you "ought to be." Use it to help your fiancé(e) understand you, and to help you understand your fiancé(e).

Commonly Observed Differences in Sexuality		
	Men	Women
Attitude	Physical Compartmentalized	Relational Wholistic
Stimulation	Body-centered Sight Smell Actions	Person-centered Touch Attitudes Words
Needs	Respect To be physically needed Physical expression	Respect To be emotionally needed Relational intimacy

Commonly Observed Differences in Sexuality		
	Men	Women
Sexual Response	Acyclical Quick excitement Difficult to distract	Cyclical Slow excitement Easily distracted
Orgasm	Shorter, more intense More physically oriented	Longer, more in-depth More emotionally oriented

7. What potential sexual problems can be anticipated in a marriage because men are generally more oriented toward the physical act of sex while women are more relationally oriented? How can you address these differences?

_____

_____

_____

_____

_____

8. Why is it important for men to realize that women usually require more time to become sexually aroused?

_____

_____

_____

_____

9. Why is it important for women to realize the deep desire within men to be physically needed?

_____

_____

_____

_____

A Most Incredible Gift

In the context of a satisfying marriage relationship, sex serves as a reinforcing bond, just as builders use steel rods to reinforce concrete. It is the most personal and private act husbands and wives can share, a celebration of their unity and oneness.

Sex in marriage is the physical expression of what is true of a couple on the emotional, mental and spiritual levels. It is the gift God has given to a husband and wife to communicate love and to demonstrate emotional and spiritual oneness on a physical plane.

Because this bonding between a husband and wife is so powerful, breaking that bond through infidelity can cause devastating damage to a marriage. And because our culture is so saturated with sex, it is critical for you and your spouse to do what you can to protect your relationship—to protect the gift God gives you.

NAVIGATING BY
TRUE NORTH:
Truths to Chart Your Course

♥ Because sex is God's idea, growing in your relationship with Him is the most important thing you can do to develop your sex life.

♥ Sex is not an act, but a process of intimate communication.

♥ God's purposes for sex are: procreation, pleasure and protection.

♥ Understanding and discussing expectations will alleviate fears, disarm potential bombshells and head potential conflicts off at the pass.

♥ Understanding your differences, as male and female, is foundational to developing a healthy, mutually satisfying sex life.

♥ Sex in marriage is best compared to a thermometer, not a thermostat. It is the physical *expression* of what is true of a couple on the emotional, mental, physical and spiritual levels. It is not a thermostat that, if turned up, will warm up your relationship.

Note
1. Louis H. Evans, Jr., *Hebrews: The Communicator's Commentary Series* (Waco, TX: Word Publishing, 1985), p. 243.

Couple's Project

What temptations do you need to avoid?

 GET REAL

1. Spend a few minutes going through "Get the Picture" and "Get the Truth," sharing and discussing your answers to the different questions. Be sure to ask your fiancé(e) to explain the answers.

2. From your observations of the chart on page 215 on commonly observed differences in sexuality, complete the following phrase individually and then share your answers with each other:

   What I need you to understand about me from this chart is that because I am a man/woman . . .

   _____

   _____

   _____

   _____

   _____

   _____

   _____

3. Individually, write down three things you are eagerly antic-
   ipating in your sexual relationship and three things you
   are anxious about.

Anticipation	Anxiety

    a. Share your answers with each other.

    b. Ask your fiancé(e) what you can do now, or later, to
   alleviate or address the most pressing anxiety issue.

4. Which one of the following weather phenomena best expresses what you anticipate your honeymoon night will
   be like?

    ❏ **A tornado**: Focused, fast moving, intense, wild and
   unpredictable

    ❏ **A hurricane**: Powerful, methodical, slow moving,
   calm surrounded by incredible turbulence

    ❏ **A blizzard**: Wind chill at 20 degrees below zero,
   everything comes to a standstill, whipping sleet followed by pristine wispy blankets of sparkling snow

    ❏ **A thunderstorm**: A little of everything—lightning,
   thunder, wind, rain and hail

    ❏ **Heat lightning**: Electrical fireworks off in the dis-
   tance but nothing really happens where you are

    ❏ **Soaking rain**: A cold, depressing shower that damp-
   ens your enthusiasm

a. Explain your answer to your fiancé(e).

b. Discuss any differing expectations you may have.

5. What are the most important insights you have gained from this chapter about God's design for sexual intimacy?

_____

_____

_____

_____

_____

_____

 GET DEEPER

For more information on starting out your marriage right in this area, read:

Sexual Intimacy in Marriage, by William Cutrer and Sandra Glahn

Intended for Pleasure, by Ed and Gaye Wheat

 GET TO THE HEART
of Your Marriage

Making Prayer a Priority Commitment

Probably no other spiritual discipline has encouraged intimacy between a man and woman in marriage more than prayer. Daily prayer together as a couple will result in innumerable benefits to you as a couple. One of those benefits is emotional closeness that enables a couple to connect to their God and one another on a daily basis. When we pray with and for one another, it demands that we have forgiven one another.

Prayer together enhances not only spiritual and emotional oneness, but also physical oneness.

Would you be willing to commit to your fiancé(e) that you will pray together daily? If so, write out a commitment to God that both of you will sign.

OUR PRAYER COMMITMENT

_____

_____

_____

_____

_____

_____

_____

_____

_____ Date _____

_____ Date _____

SPECIAL QUESTIONS
for Those Who Were Previously Married

Answer these questions individually, then share your answers with your fiancé(e).

1. How are you going to handle comparison to your previous spouse in this area?

   _____

   _____

   _____

   _____

2. List any wounds (emotional, physical, spiritual, mental) that you need to work through personally and with your fiancé(e).

   _____

   _____

   _____

   _____

3. Ask your fiancé(e) what his or her questions or fears are concerning this area of your future marriage in light of your previous marriage. Record your answers and talk about how you can work through these issues.

   _____

   _____

   _____

   _____

 A SPECIAL MESSAGE
on Sharing the Past with Your Fiancé(e)

As you contemplate marriage, you may look back with regret and guilt at sexual choices you've made in the past. And you may wonder, *Just how much of the past do I need to share with my fiancé(e)?*

This is not an easy question to answer, for several reasons:

♥ Sharing your past mistakes and sins may lead to several days of shame-filled, painful moments between you as a couple.

♥ It may mean reliving incidents you'd rather not remember.

♥ It may result in a broken engagement.

You may be tempted to avoid sharing anything from your past; after all, as a Christian, your sins are forgiven at the cross, and the Bible says, "there is now no condemnation to those who are in Christ Jesus" (Rom. 8:1).

And while these things are true spiritually in our relationship with God, there are consequences of past sins that need to be honestly dealt with as a couple moves toward marriage. While you do not need to share every detail, you cannot avoid the fact that your life has been shaped by your choices. If you and your fiancé(e) desire to make a solid decision about marriage, you need to be honest with each other and deal with your pasts. It is better to speak the truth prior to your marriage than to live with the fear, deceit and shame that come from hiding the truth from your spouse.

There is one other benefit to sharing your past. True healing can occur when you confess your sins to one another. God has used marriage to heal individuals from past hurts that have haunted them for years. This is especially true when dealing with sexual immorality. Many men and women have found forgiveness, grace and liberty by confessing these scarring circumstances to their would-be spouses.

These are not easy issues to discuss. And there is no cookie-cutter set of solutions to what you may be struggling with. In an effort to guide those who are struggling with knowing what to do and how to go about it, however, here are some principles and perspectives:

If You Are Burdened with Something You Feel You Should Tell Your Fiancé(e):

1. Write out a list of all that you are feeling a need to share with your fiancé(e). (Not in great detail—just a list of events, choices or hurts you've experienced.) The list will most likely contain things you've done or that have happened to you that you now regret.

2. Once you've completed your list, make sure you have experienced God's forgiveness and cleansing for everything you've written. If you have not, spend some time in prayer, repenting and confessing your sin. You will experience God's forgiveness on the basis of 1 John 1:9, which tells us, "If we confess our sins, he is faithful and just and will forgive us our sins and purify us from all unrighteousness" (*NIV*).

3. Determine which items on your list you should discuss with your fiancé(e), and why. If you have doubts about any items, make sure you seek wise and godly counsel before talking with your fiancé(e). Another person's compassionate, listening ear and prayerful concern can guide you before and after you marry.

4. Set a time and place to talk with your fiancé(e). Choose a private setting where you are both free to express your emotions.

5. Before you meet, pray that your fiancé(e) will have the strength and grace to respond in a loving manner. But don't go into the meeting expecting immediate forgiveness; your fiancé(e) may need time to work through emotions and think about what he or she hears.

6. As you talk with your fiancé(e), explain why you think it's important to share these choices from your past. But avoid

sharing more than is necessary. Be careful about sharing too many explicit details, as this can become a problem later in your marriage. By going into too much detail you may give the one you love too much of the picture. Avoid morbid curiosity.

7. Give your fiancé(e) the time he or she needs to process this new information. This process may include hurt, anger or withdrawal.

8. If it becomes apparent that either of you cannot get beyond the hurt caused by relating this information, seek wise counsel together or individually. If forgiveness and reconciliation cannot occur at this point, then we suggest delaying the wedding or breaking the engagement. If God is calling you to marriage, then His perfect love will be manifested in your hearts for one another. And the Scriptures tell us, "Perfect love casts out fear" (1 John 4:18).

If You Are Hearing a Confession from Your Fiancé(e):

First, make an effort to really hear what your fiancé(e) is sharing. Ask yourself, "Why did he (she) come to me with this?" Look beyond the past and its ugliness to the broken heart that is sharing.

Second, consider your own condition before God—a sinner saved by grace. We are all flawed as humans. Because we don't love perfectly, because we can have pride that we deserve "perfection," we can be tempted to condemn another for a past failure, whereas God calls us to forgive one another.

While you may legitimately decide that, given this new information about your fiancé(e), marriage is not wise, don't let pride prevent you from responding with love and forgiveness when your fiancé(e) is willing to share the mistakes from the past.

Where Do We Go from Here?

Congratulations on completing *Preparing for Marriage*! You've worked hard to reach this point, and we trust that God has used this process to draw you closer to Him and to each other. If He is leading you to marry, the principles you've learned here and the communication experienced will provide the foundation for a oneness marriage.

Turn to chapter 3, which guides you through the process of making your decision about marriage. If you have not completed the Couple's Project, do so now. If you have worked through it, take a moment to look over your answers. Do you still have the same convictions about your fiancé(e) and about your marriage?

Are you ready to receive your fiancé(e) as God's provision for you? If so, sign the following statement and date it:

I can wholeheartedly receive

_____

as God's perfect provision for a lifetime.

_____ Date _____

Building a Marriage on the Rock

In this workbook we have encouraged you to follow God's blueprint for marriage found in the Bible. Here are a few suggestions for building your relationship as you begin your life together:

1. In Matthew 7:24-27, Jesus speaks of the wisdom of following God's Word:

    Therefore everyone who hears these words of mine and puts them into practice is like a wise man who built his house on the rock. The rain came down, the streams rose, and the winds blew and beat against that house; yet it did not fall, because it had its foundation on the rock. But everyone who hears these words of mine and does not put them into practice is like a foolish man who built his house on sand. The rain came down, the streams rose, and the winds blew and beat against that house, and it fell with a great crash (*NIV*).

A life and a marriage built upon the rock of God's Word will withstand whatever storms you face in life. You may not realize it, but by completing this workbook, you've been building on that rock—you've studied and discussed Scriptures together, you've prayed together and you've talked about how you can walk with God together. We hope you've received a taste of marriage as a spiritual relationship between a man, a woman and God. Our prayer is that you continue this experience by regularly spending time together in the Word and in prayer.

2. Remember that one of the greatest enemies of your marriage is your natural selfishness—your sin. Each day you will be tempted to get your way and to manipulate your spouse to help meet your needs and fulfill your desires. But the Christian life, lived in submission to Christ, is one

of servanthood and setting aside your desires. Commit to dying daily to your sin.

3. Select a Scripture verse that you will build upon as a verse for your future marriage and family. For example, one couple chose Proverbs 3:3, which says, "Do not let kindness and truth leave you; bind them around your neck, write them on the tablet of your heart." They took the words "kindness" and "truth" and had them inscribed in each of their wedding rings. These two words serve as reminders to them of the pillars they want their home to be founded on for a lifetime.

4. Deuteronomy 24:5 says:

When a man takes a new wife, he shall not go out with the army nor be charged with any duty; he shall be free at home one year and shall give happiness to his wife whom he has taken.

While you may not be in the military, you would be wise to take the advice of this passage and devote the first year of your marriage to developing your relationship. Make a habit of saying no to many of your activities, and say yes often to being with each other the first year. You will have a lifetime after the first year to focus on others. This will build a solid base for your marriage.

5. Many of the principles found in this workbook are taken from the Weekend to Remember marriage conference and from studies in the HomeBuilders Couples Series. If you have the opportunity to attend a conference or one of these home Bible studies in your city, take it! Visit www.familylife.com for more information.

6. On your wedding day, you will likely recite vows that read much like those used by couples for centuries:

I, _____,
take you _____,
to be my (wife/husband), to have and to hold from
this day forward, for better or for worse, for richer, for
poorer, in sickness and in health, to love and to cher-
ish; from this day forward until death do us part.

Like many other couples, you may have little idea what
those vows truly mean right now. But in the future months
and years, you will have the opportunity to learn firsthand
what it means to stay together "for better or for worse, for
richer, for poorer, in sickness and in health." You will experience all of life together, and at times you will wonder if you
really have the power to make your marriage work.

Remember that the real joy of marriage comes in working
through all that life throws at you, and doing it together. And
remember that you truly can't do it alone. The God who created marriage also gives us the power—through the Holy
Spirit—to live according to His Word and to build the type of
marriage you dream of. As Paul wrote in Philippians 4:13, "I
can do all things through Him who strengthens me."

That power is available to you, and it makes all the difference.

Bonus: Parental Wisdom Questionnaire

*My son, observe the commandment of your father and
do not forsake the teaching of your mother.*

PROVERBS 6:20

*Honor your father and your mother, that your days may be
prolonged in the land which the LORD your God gives you.*

EXODUS 20:12

This project is designed to help you accomplish two things.

First, it will help you honor your parents by seeking their advice and counsel. The process of asking your parents these questions also offers you the insight and wisdom of those who know you best (or at least the longest). Keep in mind that as an adult, you are responsible for your own decisions in life. You are not asking your parents to make the decision about getting married. You are gaining their input, insights and counsel.

Second, it will help you honor your future in-laws by involving them in the process of helping you understand how to love their child. Your relationship with your in-laws can be one of the richest in your life when you start out your marriage by honoring them.

Special note: This project is designed for couples that are already engaged. If you are still deciding whether to get married, we suggest completing this at a later date when the questions would be more appropriate.

Instructions

We suggest three options for completing this project. Choose the one that best fits your situation.

> OPTION A: Send the questionnaire to your parents and to your future in-laws along with a stamped return envelope. Include a cover letter explaining the project. Ask them to return their answers to you within one or two weeks of receiving it.

> OPTION B: Set aside a time when you can call your parents and your in-laws to go through the questionnaire over the phone. Be sure to give them ample time to think about their answers. You may want to send them the questions beforehand so they can think about and discuss their answers.

> OPTION C: Arrange to have a meal, dessert or coffee with your parents to administer the questionnaire. Let them know the questions beforehand so they can be thinking about their answers. Ask your parents their questions first, then your fiancé(e) can ask the "in-law" questions.

Special Instructions

1. If your parents or in-laws are divorced, talk over with your fiancé(e) how you should proceed. You may want to ask these questions of step-parents if you have a strong relationship, or you may want to only ask your biological parents. We believe that the more parents are involved in this project the better. However, you must decide what is appropriate and best for you at this time.

2. Feel free to eliminate or adapt the questionnaire if you sense that certain questions may be difficult or awkward for a parent to answer.

3. We understand that many who marry today come from difficult family backgrounds. The tragic consequences of alcoholism, abuse, neglect and alienation follow many young people into their marriage. If this is your situation, you may decide it is not appropriate to complete this project.

Whatever your relationship with your parents, God's Word calls you to honor them. A very helpful resource that can give you perspective and hope is *The Best Gift You Can Give Your Parents*, by Dennis Rainey. The book provides some helpful insights and practical examples for those from difficult family backgrounds.

Parental Wisdom Questionnaire

Answer the following questions as if your child is asking them. If you are unable to answer a question, feel free to move to the next one.

1. What *strengths* do you see in my life that will help me in marriage?

   _____

   _____

   _____

   _____

2. What weaknesses do you see in my life that will be a challenge for me to work on and overcome in my marriage?

   _____

   _____

   _____

   _____

   _____

3. If you could give me one piece of advice about marriage (based on what you did right or wrong), what would it be and why?

   _____

   _____

   _____

   _____

4. What is your best advice to me in the following areas as I embark on this new adventure called marriage? (Pick three to five that you would like to comment on.)

Finances:

_____

_____

_____

_____

_____

_____

_____

Communication:

_____

_____

_____

_____

_____

_____

_____

Sex:

_____

_____

_____

_____

_____

_____

Husband/Wife roles:

_____

_____

_____

_____

_____

_____

Commitment:

_____
_____
_____
_____
_____

Humor:

_____
_____
_____
_____
_____

Being a parent:

_____
_____
_____
_____
_____

Spiritual growth:

_____
_____
_____
_____
_____

Priorities in life:

_____
_____
_____

_____
_____
_____

Work:

_____
_____
_____
_____
_____

5. If you could keep just one memory, one experience of time together in all your married life, what would it be and why?

_____
_____
_____
_____
_____

6. Is there anything special or meaningful to you that you would like us to include in the wedding ceremony?

_____
_____
_____
_____
_____

7. How do you anticipate that my relationship with you, as my parents, will change now that I am marrying and establishing a new family and home?

_____
_____
_____
_____

8. How would you want us to handle holidays?

_____

_____

_____

_____

_____

_____

9. If God gives us children, how involved would you like to be in their lives?

_____

_____

_____

_____

_____

_____

10. Would you like us to drop in unannounced or call before visiting?

_____

_____

_____

_____

_____

_____

11. Do you have any specific expectations about where we attend church?

_____

_____

_____

_____

_____

Answer these questions as if your future son-in-law or daughter-in-law is asking them:

1. What are some qualities you see in me, or know about me, that make you think I am the right person for your son/daughter to marry?

   _____

   _____

   _____

   _____

   _____

   _____

   _____

   _____

2. What unique and personal advice would you give me about your son/daughter that will help me be the life partner he/she needs?

   _____

   _____

   _____

   _____

   _____

   _____

   _____

   _____

3. How would you like for me to address you after we are married?

   _____

   _____

   _____

   _____

   _____

   _____

Appendix B

Bonus: Couple Interview

Hearing from others who have gone before you is one of the most rewarding and beneficial things you can do for your engagement and your marriage. This project will help you do just that. You are going to discover what seeds you need to be planting now to have a colorful, fragrant and vibrant marriage 5, 10 and 20 years down the road.

Instructions

1. Complete this interview with your mentor couple or with another married couple (married at least five years) that you both respect and admire. If you chose someone besides your mentors, ask this couple if they would spend some time with you to complete an interview that is part of your premarital counseling. Explain that the interview consists of seven questions about marriage and family life. The questions are simple and straightforward, so they won't need any preparation time.

2. Conduct the interview over a meal, dessert or coffee. You may want to take turns asking the questions. If you have other questions you'd like to ask them, be sure to ask their permission.

3. Remember to employ the communication skills you have just learned.

> ♥ Ask clarifying and summary questions
> ♥ Listen for the "total message" (words, tone, nonverbal cues)

4. Take notes. The insights you gain in this time will be invaluable.

Interview Questions

Looking Back

1. Describe how you met and got engaged.

   What was life like for you?

   What attracted you to each other?

   How did you propose?

   What were some of the emotions you felt at various points in the process?

2. What are some of the fondest memories you have of your first years of marriage? Why?

3. What were the greatest areas of conflict or tension in your first few years of marriage? How did you handle them?

4. How has your relationship with God affected your communication with one another?

Looking at the Present

5. What have you learned about your spouse that has been most helpful to you as you seek to understand and love each other?

6. What are the greatest areas of conflict in your marriage today?

   What spiritual principles have been most helpful to you in solving these tensions?

7. How do you manage schedules, work demands and outside activities while maintaining family as a priority?

8. What are some practical ways you have found to keep your relationship with God a priority in your marriage and family?

Looking Ahead

9. What advice would you give us today that you think will make the greatest difference in our marriage 20 years from now?

Appendix C

Our Problems, God's Answers

Every couple eventually has to deal with problems in their relationship. Communication problems. Money problems. Difficulties with sexual intimacy. Working on these issues is important to cultivating a strong, loving relationship.

One basic problem is at the heart of every issue in every relationship, and it's a problem we can't help you fix. No matter how hard you try, this problem is too big for you to handle on your own.

The problem is separation from God. If you want to experience marriage the way it was designed to be, *you need a vital relationship with the God who created you and offers you the power to live a life of joy and purpose.*

Falling Short

What separates us from God is one more problem—sin. Many people today do not understand what "sin" is. They may assume that the term refers to a list of bad habits or behaviors that everyone agrees are wrong, like the 10 Commandments. If they recognize how their behaviors are hurting others, they may vow to work hard to become better people.

But if we are honest with ourselves, we know that our sin problem runs much deeper than a list of bad habits. We know that, in our hearts, we are self-centered human beings who want to fulfill our desires and live life the way we want. We're most concerned with getting what we want.

The root problem is that all of us have rebelled against God. We have ignored Him and have decided to run our own lives in a way that makes sense to us. The Bible says that the God who created us wants us to follow His plans for our lives. But because of our sin problem, we think our ideas and plans are better than His.

> For all have sinned and fall short of the glory of God (Rom. 3:23).

What does it mean to "fall short of the glory of God"? It means that none of us has trusted and treasured God the way we should. We have sought to satisfy ourselves with other things and have treated those things as more valuable than God. We have gone our own way. According to the Bible, we have to pay a penalty for our sin. We cannot simply do things the way we choose and hope it will all be okay with God. Following our own plan leads to our destruction.

> There is a way which seems right to a man, but its end is the way to death (Prov. 14:12).

> For the wages of sin is death (Rom. 6:23a).

The penalty for sin is that we are forever separated from God's love. God is holy, and we are sinful. No matter how hard we try, we cannot come up with some plan, like living a good life or even trying to do what the Bible says, and hope that we can avoid the penalty.

God's Solution to Sin

Thankfully, God has a way to solve our dilemma. He became a man through the person of Jesus Christ. He lived a holy life, in perfect obedience to God's plan. He also willingly died on a cross to pay our penalty for sin. Then He proved that He is more powerful than sin or death by rising from the dead. He alone has the power to overrule the penalty for our sin.

Jesus said to him, "I am the way, and the truth, and the life; no one comes to the Father but through me" (John 14:6).

But God shows his love for us in that while we were still sinners, Christ died for us (Rom. 5:8, *ESV*).

Christ died for our sins . . . he was buried . . . he was raised on the third day . . . he appeared to Cephas [Peter], then to the twelve. Then he appeared to more than five hundred (1 Cor. 15:3-6, *ESV*).

For the wages of sin is death, but the free gift of God is eternal life in Christ Jesus our Lord (Rom. 6:23).

The death and resurrection of Jesus has fixed our sin problem. He has bridged the gap between God and us. He is calling all of us to come to Him and to give up our own flawed plan for how to run our lives. He wants us to trust God and His plan.

Accepting God's Solution

If you agree that you are separated from God, He is calling you to confess your sins. All of us have made messes of our lives because we have stubbornly preferred our ideas and plans over His. As a result, we deserve to be cut off from God's love and His care for us. But God has promised that if we will agree that we have rebelled against His plan for us and have messed up our lives, He will forgive us and will fix our sin problem.

But to all who did receive him, who believed in his name, he gave the right to become children of God (John 1:12, *ESV*).

For by grace you have been saved through faith. And this is not your own doing; it is the gift of God, not a result of works, so that no one may boast (Eph. 2:8-9, *ESV*).

When the Bible talks about receiving Christ, it means we acknowledge that we are sinners and that we can't fix the problem ourselves. It means we turn away from our sin. And it means we trust Christ to forgive our sins and make us the kind of people He wants us to be. It's not enough to just intellectually believe that Christ is the Son of God. We must trust in Him and His plan for our lives by faith, as an act of the will.

Are things right between you and God, with Him and His plan at the center of your life? Or is life spinning out of control as you seek to make your way on your own?

You can decide today to make a change. You can turn to Christ and allow Him to transform your life. All you need to do is talk to Him and tell Him what is stirring in your mind and in your heart. If you've never done this, consider taking the steps listed here:

- Do you agree that you need God? Tell God.
- Have you made a mess of your life by following your own plan? Tell God.
- Do you want God to forgive you? Tell God.
- Do you believe that Jesus' death on the cross and His resurrection from the dead gave Him the power to fix your sin problem and to grant you the free gift of eternal life? Tell God.
- Are you ready to acknowledge that God's plan for your life is better than any plan you could come up with? Tell God.
- Do you agree that God has the right to be the Lord and master of your life? Tell God.

Seek the LORD while He may be found; call upon Him while He is near (Isa. 55:6).

The following is a suggested prayer:

Lord Jesus, I need You. Thank You for dying on the cross for my sins. I receive You as my Savior and Lord. Thank

*You for forgiving my sins and giving me eternal life. Make
me the kind of person You want me to be.*

Living the Christian Life

For a person who is a follower of Christ—a Christian—the
penalty for sin is paid in full. But the effect of sin continues
throughout our lives.

> If we say we have no sin, we deceive ourselves, and the
> truth is not in us (1 John 1:8, *ESV*).

> For I do not do the good I want, but the evil I do not
> want is what I keep on doing (Rom. 7:19, *ESV*).

The effects of sin carry over into our marriages as well. Even
Christians struggle to maintain solid, God-honoring marriages. Most couples eventually realize they can't do it on their
own. But with God's help, they can succeed. The Holy Spirit
can have a huge impact in the marriages of Christians who live
constantly, moment by moment, under His gracious direction.

Self-centered Christians

Many Christians struggle to live the Christian life in their own
strength because they are not allowing God to direct their
lives. Their interests are self-directed, often resulting in failure
and frustration.

> But I, brothers, could not address you as spiritual peo-
> ple, but as people of the flesh, as infants in Christ. I
> fed you with milk, not solid food, for you were not
> ready for it. And even now you are not ready, for you
> are still of the flesh. For while there is jealousy and
> strife among you, are you not of the flesh and behav-
> ing only in a human way? (1 Cor. 3:1-3, *ESV*).

The self-centered Christian cannot experience the abundant and fruitful Christian life. Such people trust in their own efforts to live the Christian life. They are either uninformed about—or have forgotten—God's love, forgiveness and power. This kind of Christian:

♥ has an up-and-down spiritual experience
♥ cannot understand himself—he wants to do what is right, but cannot
♥ fails to draw upon the power of the Holy Spirit to live the Christian life

Some or all of the following traits may characterize the Christian who does not fully trust God:

Disobedience	**Jealous**
Lack of love for God and others	Worrisome
Inconsistent prayer life	**Critical**
Lack of desire for Bible study	Lack of purpose
Legalistic attitude	**Easily discouraged,**
Plagued by impure thoughts	**frustrated**

Note: The individual who professes to be a Christian but who continues to practice sin should realize that he may not be a Christian at all, according to 1 John 2:3; 3:6,9; Ephesians 5:5.

Spirit-centered Christians

When a Christian puts Christ on the throne of his life, he yields to God's control. This Christian's interests are directed by the Holy Spirit, resulting in harmony with God's plan.

But the fruit of the Spirit is love, joy, peace, patience, kindness, goodness, faithfulness, gentleness, self-control; against such things there is no law (Gal. 5:22–23, *ESV*).

Jesus said:

I came that they may have life and have it abundantly
(John 10:10b, *ESV*).

I am the vine; you are the branches. Whoever abides in
me and I in him, he it is that bears much fruit, for
apart from me you can do nothing (John 15:5, *ESV*).

But you will receive power when the Holy Spirit has
come upon you, and you will be my witnesses in
Jerusalem and in all Judea and Samaria, and to the end
of the earth (Acts 1:8, *ESV*).

The following traits result naturally from the Holy Spirit's
work in our lives:

Christ-centered	**Love**
Holy Spirit empowered	Joy
Motivated to tell others	**Peace**
about Jesus	Patience
Dedicated to prayer	**Kindness**
Student of	Goodness
God's Word	**Faithfulness**
Trusts God	Gentleness
Obeys God	**Self-control**

The degree to which these traits appear in a Christian's life
and marriage depends upon the extent to which the Christian
trusts the Lord with every detail of life, and upon that person's
maturity in Christ. One who is only beginning to understand
the ministry of the Holy Spirit should not be discouraged if
he is not as fruitful as mature Christians who have known and
experienced this truth for a longer period of time.

Giving God Control

Jesus promises His followers an abundant and fruitful life as they allow themselves to be directed and empowered by the Holy Spirit. As we give God control of our lives, Christ lives in and through us in the power of the Holy Spirit (see John 15).

If you sincerely desire to be directed and empowered by God, you can turn your life over to the control of the Holy Spirit right now (see Matt. 5:6; John 7:37-39).

First, confess your sins to God, agreeing with Him that you want to turn from any past sinful patterns in your life. Thank God in faith that He has forgiven all of your sins because Christ died for you (see Col. 2:13-15; 1 John 1:9; 2:1-3; Heb. 10:1-18).

Be sure to offer every area of your life to God (see Rom. 12:1-2). Consider what areas you might rather keep to yourself, and be sure you're willing to give God control in those areas.

By faith, commit yourself to living according to the Holy Spirit's guidance and power.

> *Live by the Spirit:* "But I say, walk by the Spirit, and you will not gratify the desires of the flesh. For the desires of the flesh are against the Spirit, and the desires of the Spirit are against the flesh, for these are opposed to each other, to keep you from doing the things you want to do" (Gal. 5:16-17, *ESV*).

> *Trust in God's promise:* "And this is the confidence that we have toward him, that if we ask anything according to his will he hears us. And if we know that he hears us in whatever we ask, we know that we have the requests that we have asked of him" (1 John 5:14-15, *ESV*).

Expressing Your Faith Through Prayer

Prayer is one way of expressing your faith to God. If the prayer that follows expresses your sincere desire, consider praying the prayer or putting the thoughts into your own words:

Dear God, I need You. I acknowledge that I have been directing my own life and that, as a result, I have sinned against You. I thank You that You have forgiven my sins through Christ's death on the cross for me. I now invite Christ to take His place on the throne of my life. Take control of my life through the Holy Spirit as You promised You would if I asked in faith. I now thank You for directing my life and for empowering me through the Holy Spirit.

Walking in the Spirit

If you become aware of an area of your life (an attitude or an action) that is displeasing to God, simply confess your sin and thank God that He has forgiven your sins on the basis of Christ's death on the cross. Accept God's love and forgiveness by faith, and continue to have fellowship with Him.

If you find that you've taken back control of your life through sin—a definite act of disobedience—try this exercise, "Spiritual Breathing," as you give that control back to God.

- ♥ *Exhale.* Confess your sin. Agree with God that you've sinned against Him, and thank Him for His forgiveness of it, according to 1 John 1:9 and Hebrews 10:1-25. Remember that confession involves repentance, a determination to change attitudes and actions.

- ♥ *Inhale.* Surrender control of your life to Christ, inviting the Holy Spirit to once again take charge. Trust that He now directs and empowers you, according to the command of Galatians 5:16-17 and the promise of 1 John 5:14-15. Returning to your faith in God enables you to continue to experience God's love and forgiveness.

Revolutionizing Your Marriage

This new commitment of your life to God will enrich your marriage. Sharing with your spouse what you've committed

to is a powerful step in strengthening your faith. As you ex-
hibit the Holy Spirit's work within you, your spouse may be
drawn to make the same commitment you've made. If both of
you have given control of your lives to the Holy Spirit, you'll be
able to help each other remain true to God, and your marriage
may be revolutionized. With God in charge, life becomes an
amazing adventure.

About the Writers

David Boehi is a senior editor at FamilyLife. He is editor of the HomeBuilders Couples Series and writes and edits articles for FamilyLife's website, blogs, and e-newsletters. He and his wife, Merry, have two children and live in Little Rock, Arkansas.

Jeff Schulte is a fellow and director of the Sage Hill Institute, an initiative for authentic Christian leadership, and speaks nationally and internationally on biblical masculinity, fatherhood, spiritual formation, leadership and relational authenticity. He is a graduate of Yale University and earned two masters degrees from Western Seminary. He and his wife, Brenda, have six children.

Lloyd Shadrach is a teaching pastor at Fellowship Bible Church in Brentwood, Tennessee, which he co-planted in 1997. Previously he was a staff member with FamilyLife for 13 years. Lloyd is a graduate of Dallas Theological Seminary. He and his wife, Lisa, live in Franklin, Tennessee, with their three children.

Brent Nelson has served with a variety of ministries, including FamilyLife and Athletes in Action. He has earned degrees at Trinity College, Indiana University, and Trinity Evangelical Divinity School. He and his wife, Cassandra, live in Columbia, Tennessee, with their three children.

Dennis Rainey, general editor, is the president and cofounder of FamilyLife, a division of Campus Crusade for Christ. Dennis serves as the daily host of the radio program *FamilyLife Today*. He and his wife, Barbara, agree that their proudest achievement is their six children and many grandchildren. The Raineys live in Little Rock, Arkansas.